Progressive Plyometrics for Kids

DVD INCLUDED

Donald A. Chu
Avery D. Faigenbaum
Jeff E. Falkel

HEALTHY LEARNING™

ISBN: 1-58518-955-3
Library of Congress Control Number: 2005938380
Cover design: Jeanne Hamilton
Diagrams: Chasity Siebert and Jeanne Hamilton
Book layout: Jeanne Hamilton
Front cover photo: Brennan Tiffany and James Marsh

Healthy Learning
P.O. Box 1828
Monterey, CA 93942
www.healthylearning.com

This book is dedicated to all the young aspiring athletes who have participated in our strength and conditioning programs over the past 30 years. Your enthusiasm to train, eagerness to learn, willingness to work hard, and commitment to athleticism continue to make us better coaches. Thanks to you, more people than ever before now understand that progressive plyometric training can be a safe, effective, and worthwhile method of conditioning for youth. We thank you for helping us develop the vision for this text, which will help teachers and coaches develop the essential knowledge and teaching skills to safely and effectively instruct children and teenagers.

Dedication

Acknowledgments

First of all, we want to thank all the boys and girls who have participated in our programs over the years that have taught us that physical activity is a great way to have fun, make friends, and learn something new. We also want to thank the teachers, coaches, and therapists who we have worked with and who believe that a progressive plyometric training program can be safe, effective, and worthwhile for boys and girls of all abilities. We especially want to thank the "stars" of the book and DVD, Hunter Baird, Jenny Rivera, and Marcelis Short, for their hard work and a lot of fun. We thank Dr. Jim Peterson, Kristi Huelsing, the staff at Coaches Choice/Healthy Learning, our photographer Chris Gage, and our videographer, Mike March, for making this project a reality, as well as for all of your support, help, and encouragement along the journey. And we want to acknowledge the efforts of Mr. Jim McFarland, from Hillsborough High School in New Jersey, who helped us evaluate the efficacy of our youth conditioning programs.

Several years ago, the authors got together to create a comprehensive, progressive program of plyometric exercises specifically designed for youth. We decided that rather than listing drills we have used successfully in the past, we would design a program that was progressive, easy to implement, cost effective, and developmentally appropriate for all children and teenagers regardless of their athletic ability. Our book is based on our firm belief that a progressive plyometric program can not only enhance athletic performance, but can also develop fundamental fitness abilities such as speed, agility, power, strength, and flexibility in youth.

Plyometrics are dynamic exercises that elite athletes have used for decades as part of their training programs. Our book is based on the scientific principles of plyometric training, but modified for boys and girls who are physically and psychologically less mature. While plyometrics were once thought of as inappropriate, if not unsafe, for use with young athletes, our clinical observations, years of coaching experience, and scientific research studies have shown that plyometric training can be a safe, effective, and worthwhile method of conditioning for children and adolescents. Since 1972, thousands of aspiring young athletes as well as elite competitors have benefited from participation in our progressive plyometric programs. While youth in our conditioning programs enhanced their physical fitness and gained confidence in their abilities to perform plyometric drills, communicating with the young participants in our programs has reinforced the importance of keeping our youth programs progressive and enjoyable.

It has been our collective experiences that have provided us with the foundation upon which to develop our progressive plyometric program. Once we observed that a well-designed plyometric training program could be safe and worthwhile for youth, we actually evaluated the efficacy of our training methods throughout the United States. Our findings challenged common misconceptions and provided reassurance that plyometric training can be part of a child's multifaceted conditioning program. For example, our research indicates that dynamic warm-up protocols are more effective for preparing youth for sport activities than a more traditional approach of static stretching. We have also observed that participation in a progressive plyometric program is essential for optimizing power performance in youth.

All youth in our after-school programs, fitness classes, and sport-training programs perform some type of plyometric training as part of their conditioning program. However, plyometrics should not be haphazardly programmed nor should youth follow adult training guidelines. The key to safe and effective youth programming is to appreciate the fact that kids are active like adults, but kids are active in different ways and for different reasons. When combined with enthusiasm and a zest for learning, our book will provide you with all the information you need to make plyometric training an enjoyable and worthwhile experience for children and adolescents. We have also included a DVD with our book that describes each of the exercises in greater detail to help athletes perform them correctly. The DVD also features coaching points for every drill to assist coaches, teachers, and parents. We hope that you will enjoy reading this book as much as we enjoyed consolidating our years of experience and research into book form.

Contents

1

Understanding Plyometrics

Progressive Plyometrics Success Story

Chris was a young athlete with amazing straight-ahead speed, but had difficulty stopping and changing directions. Once he got going, few people could catch him. However, when he had to change direction or decelerate and then accelerate again, he was not nearly as fast. We started him on our progressive plyometric program, and after only a few weeks his ability to quickly change directions, stop and start, and rapidly get back up to his speed dramatically improved.

You picked up this book on plyometric training because you have at least heard about this type of exercise. You may have read about plyometric training in a fitness book or seen adult athletes performing these drills on television. The bottom line is that coaches are talking about plyometrics and athletes in nearly all sports are benefiting from this type of training. But along with this growth in popularity has come many questions. How do plyometrics work? Do they really enhance speed and power? And are plyometrics safe for children and teenagers? In this book we will dispel the misperceptions associated with plyometric training and provide you with reassurance that a progressive plyometric program can be a safe, worthwhile, and fun method of training for boys and girls of all abilities. We will help you understand the essentials of plyometric training and provide you with a simple yet effective conditioning program that can be incorporated into any child's physical activity program.

What are Plyometrics?

Plyometrics—first known simply as "jump training"—refer to a type of exercise that links strength with speed of movement to produce power. In fact, if a muscle group contracts rapidly after previously lengthening, the associated exercise can be called plyometric. Simply stated, the term plyometrics literally means to increase measurement (plio = more; metric = measure). Unlike a bike ride or a traditional strength-building exercise such as the bench press, a plyometric exercise enables a muscle to reach maximal force in the shortest possible time. Plyometrics condition the body through dynamic movements that involve a rapid stretch of a muscle (called an eccentric muscle action), which is immediately followed by a rapid shortening of the same muscle (called a concentric muscle action). Although both muscle actions are important for the performance of any plyometric drill, the amount of time it takes to change direction from the eccentric muscle action to the concentric muscle action is a critical factor in plyometric training. This time period is called the amortization phase and should be as short as possible (ideally less than 0.1 second). Exercises performed slowly with a long amortization phase are not considered plyometric.

> Amortization phase: Time between eccentric and concentric muscle actions
>
> Concentric muscle action: Muscle shortening
>
> Eccentric muscle action: Muscle lengthening
>
> Isometric muscle action: Muscle length remains constant
>
> Plyometric: A type of exercise that involves a quick, powerful movement using a pre-stretch
>
> Strength training: A specialized type of exercise that involves the use of progressive resistance
>
> Stretch-shortening cycle: A sequence of eccentric, isometric, and concentric muscle actions

Figure 1-1. Definitions of common terms

When the stretching and shortening of a muscle is performed quickly, the nerves fire and the force generated during the muscle action is greater than the force that would be generated if the muscle was not stretched immediately before the muscle action. The rapid stretching and shortening of a muscle during a plyometric exercise is referred to as a stretch-shortening cycle (Figure 1-2). The rapid stretch that occurs immediately before the muscle shortens is called a pre-stretch and it is during this phase that elastic energy is stored in the muscle.

As an example, think about a young volleyball player who attempts to block a shot during a game. The player bends her knees and hips as she lowers her body (stretching phase), then quickly reverses direction and jumps up as high as she can to block the shot (shortening phase). This is a classic example of how the stretch-shortening cycle works. Without the rapid pre-stretch immediately preceding the shortening phase, she won't jump as high because the stored elastic energy in the muscle will waste away. To

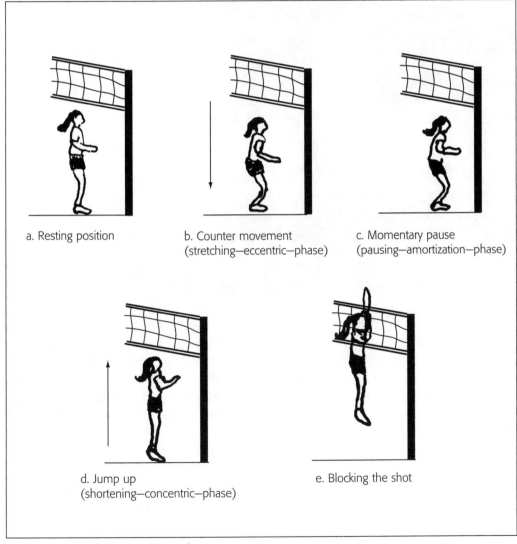

a. Resting position

b. Counter movement
(stretching—eccentric—phase)

c. Momentary pause
(pausing—amortization—phase)

d. Jump up
(shortening—concentric—phase)

e. Blocking the shot

Figure 1-2. Stretch-shortening cycle

feel the effects of the stretch-shortening cycle, stand up and get ready to jump. The first time you jump, bend your knees, stop for three to five seconds, and then jump as high as you can. The second time you jump, bend your knees and then quickly reverse direction and jump. You will jump higher during the second jump because it involves a rapid pre-stretch. Although a novice may not be able to see striking differences, with regular plyometric training, jumping ability will improve and differences in performance will become evident.

Figure 1-3. Basketball is a sport that requires all aspects of plyometric activity, such as running, jumping, and changing direction.

Research studies clearly demonstrate that plyometric training provides a distinct advantage for producing power over many other types of exercise. Even common playground activities that are considered plyometric can condition the developing muscles of boys and girls. For example, when a child plays hopscotch and jumps from square to square, the quadriceps (the front of the thigh) stretch eccentrically when the child lands, and then shorten concentrically when the child jumps. This type of exercise, although game-like in nature, actually conditions the body to increase speed of movement and improve power production. While plyometric exercises typically include hops and jumps that exploit the muscles' cycle of lengthening and shortening to increase muscle power, watching children on a playground supports the premise that the movement pattern of boys and girls as they skip and jump can be considered plyometric.

Regular participation in a progressive plyometric training program can actually make kids faster and more powerful by training the neuromuscular system to react more quickly to the stretch-shortening cycle. In essence, the goal of plyometric training is to increase the rate of stretching and shortening so that the stored elastic energy more rapidly transfers to the next explosive movement. Stated simply, muscle is made up of two genetically determined fiber types known as slow-twitch and fast-twitch fibers. Fast-twitch muscle fibers are used for short-duration, explosive movements, while slow-twitch muscle fibers are used for less intense, longer-duration muscle actions. While both slow-twitch and fast-twitch muscle fibers are important for athletes, plyometric training teaches children how to "activate" their fast-twitch muscle fibers to run faster and jump higher. Furthermore, plyometric training may actually "teach" the slow-twitch muscle fibers to behave more like fast-twitch muscle fibers.

Indeed, childhood may be the ideal time to implement some type of plyometric training program because the neuromuscular system of children is somewhat "plastic" and can therefore readily adapt to the training stress. Although adults can benefit from plyometric training, the so-called "skill-hungry" years for learning motor skills occur during childhood. As such, the nervous system of children is primed to learn motor skills that involve jumping, hopping, skipping, running, and throwing. If this window of opportunity is missed, a child who does not participate in this type of activity may not be able to catch up later on in life. In the long run, this child will be at a distinct disadvantage when the time comes to participate in more advanced training programs later in life. In our program, children develop athletic qualities and learn fundamental movement skills through creative games and activities that serve as the foundation for later sports success.

Perhaps it is not surprising to note that the best athletes in the world learn how to perform complex skills early in life. Quite frankly, it is difficult to imagine how a child who never danced could become a professional ballerina or how a teenager who never threw a ball could become a Major League baseball pitcher. Plyometric movement skills that involve the upper and lower body are extremely important in building the foundation for sports success later in life. While young athletes will get better at running and jumping by simply playing their sport, even greater gains will be made if they actually practice the skills they want to improve.

For example, virtually every young volleyball player wants to jump higher. And just by playing volleyball the jumping ability of most players will likely improve. But to maximize jumping ability young athletes need to learn how to "activate" their fast-twitch muscle fibers. Because training adaptations are specific to the movement pattern, muscles trained, and speed of movement, it is easy to see that young volleyball players who participate in a plyometric training program will become more powerful and therefore able to jump higher to block shots and score points. The bottom line is that winning is a consequence of playing well, and to play at their best, young athletes need to be prepared for the demands of sports practice and competition.

Are Plyometrics Safe for Kids?

While intuition tells you that young athletes could also benefit from plyometric training, you may have heard that plyometrics are inappropriate or even unsafe for children and teenagers. These misperceptions are categorically untrue. When well-planned and well-implemented, plyometrics can help youth develop movement competence, which can be highly beneficial to growing boys and girls. Research has demonstrated that plyometric training can increase bone strength, enhance muscular power, and improve speed and agility, and no evidence suggests that participation in a progressive plyometric training program that begins with low-intensity drills is any riskier than participation in other sports and activities. Moreover, participation in a preseason conditioning program that includes plyometric training may reduce the risk of sports-related injuries and better prepare young athletes for sports practice and competition.

Figure 1-4. With proper instruction and proper progression, plyometric exercises are safe for children.

While boys and girls have traditionally been encouraged to participate in prolonged periods of aerobic exercise such as bicycling and swimming, they have not always been encouraged to participate in plyometric training. Despite the fact that most playground games and activities can all be characterized as plyometric, some observers have a very narrow view of plyometric training and only associate drop jumps from a 32-inch box as plyometric. While this high-intensity exercise may be appropriate for elite adult athletes, literally thousands of other plyometrics exercises exist, including low-intensity double-leg hops and throws with lightweight medicine balls, both of which can be part of a youngster's fitness program.

In addition, some people recommend that individuals be able to back squat with a barbell at least one-and-a-half times their body weight before participating in a plyometric training program. However, this recommendation has not been supported by research studies and we believe this is too much weight for a child to lift before participating in a plyometric training program. Moreover, children regularly perform plyometric exercises such as jump rope and hopscotch on playgrounds every day. While participation in a well-designed youth strength-training program can certainly strengthen young muscles and connective tissues, boys and girls can begin plyometric training with low-intensity drills and gradually progress depending on needs and abilities. This is especially important for inactive boys and girls who may begin a plyometric conditioning program with suboptimal levels of strength and power. Over the years, boys and girls of all abilities have participated in our conditioning programs and not one child has experienced an exercise-related injury. This is most likely due to the well-implemented progression, competent instruction, and safe training environment that are characteristics of our youth programs.

Why Plyometrics for Kids?

Years ago we did not have to be concerned about plyometric training for boys and girls because a few hours at the local playground were more than enough to keep their bodies healthy, fit, and strong. But today, reports indicate that only about one-half of young people regularly participate in vigorous physical activity and daily enrollment in physical education classes continues to decline. Most children watch more than 20 hours of television every week, "surfing the net" has become a popular sedentary pursuit, and we chauffeur our kids everywhere. Clearly, we need to develop programs that substantially increase the amount of time children and teenagers spend running, jumping, skipping, throwing, catching, turning, and twisting. Our progressive plyometric training program provides parents, teachers and youth coaches with a safe, effective, and fun alternative to television and video games. And because children who enjoy physically activity are more likely to become adults who enjoy physical activity, our progressive plyometric program can be part of a multifaceted approach to better health.

- Increased muscle strength
- Increased muscle power
- Increased bone strength
- Improved balance
- Enhanced agility
- Increased speed
- Increased resistance to injury
- Enhanced sports performance
- A more positive attitude toward fitness activities

Figure 1-5. Potential benefits of plyometric training

Today, aspiring young athletes are often expected to train harder and longer to excel in sports, and in a growing number of cases it seems that their musculoskeletal systems are not prepared for the demands of sports practice and game situations. In some cases, it seems that parents and coaches are asking kids to play sports they are not prepared to play. In the past, kids developed general athletic qualities through free play and regular physical education. But today most kids spend more time in from of the computer or television than at the local playground.

Figure 1-6. Even the youngest child on a playground participates in plyometric exercise. Our program takes that observation and progressively increases the skill and difficulty of plyometric exercises.

We believe that most overuse injuries in youth sports are a result of a mistake in training. Training errors are a common occurrence in youth sports, and include improper preparation, poor technique, and inadequate recovery between hard training sessions. In the United States, millions of children participate in competitive sports programs as early as age five or six. But along with this staggering number of youth sport participants has come a concomitant increase in the number of sports-related injuries to ill-prepared and improperly trained young athletes. Although we genuinely appreciate the efforts of youth coaches, in some cases boys and girls are treated like miniature adults and simply asked to do too much too soon. Those of us working with young athletes are seeing a dramatic increase in the number of children and teenagers with overuse injuries such as stress fractures, bursitis, and tendonitis that are due to some repetitive pattern of overuse. The take-home message is that young athletes who possess inadequate fitness abilities are likely to become disillusioned and drop out of sports due to frustration, embarrassment, failure, and injury.

Plyometrics provide an important foundation that has been missing from the vast majority of youth training programs. While strength-training programs using weight machines and free weights (dumbbells and barbells) have proven to be beneficial for children and adolescents, plyometrics are a unique type of exercise because the drills are performed quickly and explosively. And while it makes sense that an athlete who competes at high speeds needs to train at high speeds, most activities of daily life such as walking across the room or lifting a backpack involve slow-speed movements that actually train the body to move slowly.

It is easy to understand that fast-speed training (i.e., plyometrics) should be used to prepare young athletes for fast-speed sports. For example, sports like volleyball, basketball, and football involve fast-speed movements as evidenced by athletes who regularly jump, sprint, and throw in different directions. While these young athletes will benefit from slow-speed strength training, the best youth conditioning programs involve both slow-speed and fast-speed conditioning activities. In short, asking a child to participate in a fast-speed sport without having participated in a well-designed conditioning program that includes fast-speed training is like asking a child to run before she can walk.

While factors such as poor nutrition and hard playing surfaces are recognized as risk factors for overuse injuries in children, the background level of physical activity of aspiring young athletes must also be considered. Even if a child "passes" the preparticipation medical examination in the doctor's office, that does not necessarily mean that the child's musculoskeletal system is adequately prepared for the demands of sports practice and competition. Even though some parents and youth coaches may not see the need for preseason conditioning, it may be difficult for young athletes to gain the specific benefits from an activity such as plyometrics without actually participating in a plyometric exercise program. According to the American College of Sports Medicine, up to 50% of overuse injuries sustained by young athletes could be prevented if more emphasis was placed on the development of fundamental fitness abilities prior to sports participation. We believe that most overuse injuries are due to training errors. That is, aspiring young athletes try to do too much too soon without an adequate foundation of muscle strength and power, and without adequate time for rest and recovery between workouts.

While the total elimination of sports-related injuries is an unrealistic goal, *reducing* the incidence of sports-related injuries with progressive plyometric training is a reasonable and obtainable objective. Every young athlete enters a sport with a measurable baseline level of muscular fitness. If the baseline level of fitness is equal to, or greater than, the demands required for practice and competition, the risk of injury is reduced and the likelihood of improved performance is enhanced. But if the muscular fitness base is inadequate or ill-prepared for the demands of practice and competition, injury and decreased performance may result. By strengthening the supporting structures (i.e., ligaments, tendons, and bone) and enhancing muscle performance (i.e., muscular strength, muscular endurance, and muscular power), progressive plyometric training may reduce the incidence of injuries in youth sports. Moreover, since powerful athletes are able to get to the ball before a defender, they can further reduce their risk of injury by avoiding physical contact with an opponent. All of these benefits may be of particular value to young female athletes, who appear to be at increased risk for knee injuries as compared to their young male counterparts.

Children and teenagers need to develop what we call FUNdamental fitness abilities prior to participating in sports practice and competition. Not only may the development of fundamental fitness abilities reduce the risk of injury and enable a young athlete to play the entire game, but it may also be an important factor in the development of lifelong healthy habits. In other words, proper preparation can make the difference between a positive youth sport experience and feelings of failure and low self-worth. A child's participation in sport should not start with competition, but should evolve out of preparatory conditioning that includes plyometric training. By enhancing their strength, power, speed, agility, reaction time, and balance, boys and girls will be better prepared for the demands of sports practice and competition. This is what our progressive plyometric training program is all about. It is really the development of these FUNdamental fitness abilities that influences a child's confidence (and therefore willingness) to participate in athletic activities.

Agility: The ability to quickly decelerate, change direction, and accelerate again

Balance: The maintenance and/or control of a body position

Coordination: The ability of various muscles to work together to produce a specific movement

Endurance: The capacity to continue moving for a prolonged period of time

Flexibility: The ability to move through a full range of motion

Power: The rate of performing work; the product of force and velocity

Reaction: A response to a stimulus

Speed: The ability to achieve high velocity

Strength: The maximal amount of force a muscle or muscle group can generate

---

Figure 1-7. Elements of FUNdamental fitness

For many years, some parents and youth coaches believed that the key to athletic success was for children to focus their efforts on learning and mastering the intricacies of a particular sport or sport skill instead of developing fundamental fitness abilities. But unfortunately, this shortsighted strategy limits the ability of youngsters to succeed at tasks outside of a narrow physical spectrum of a particular position or sport. Thus, some young athletes may be able to make an impressive jump shot in basketball, but may look awkward when asked to kick a soccer ball or throw a baseball. Moreover, many young athletes who participate in different sports with extended seasons never have the opportunity to engage in off-season training and enhance their fundamental fitness skills. This situation makes it difficult for these athletes to develop general athletic qualities that can serve as the foundation for more advanced training later in life.

Specializing in one sport or participating in several sports with extended competitive schedules not only limits the development of general athletic qualities, but may also lead to sports-related injuries. The bottom line is that some young athletes may need

Figure 1-8. Participation in physical activity should not begin with competitive sport, but should evolve out of preparatory conditioning that includes progressive plyometric training.

to decrease the time they spend practicing sport-specific skills to allow time for progressive physical conditioning. It is noteworthy that basketball star Michael Jordan didn't make his high school's basketball team until he was in eleventh grade and Apollo Ohno, who won silver and gold medals for short track speed skating at the Olympics, began his athletic career as a swimmer before he discovered that speed skating was an even faster form of racing.

The take-home message is that aspiring young athletes will be well-served if they spend more time developing their speed, agility, strength, and power and less time developing fancy sport skills. To the surprise of some parents, sport success as a child does not guarantee sport success as a teenager or college athlete. Children and teenage athletes need to work on their weaknesses and enhance their fundamental fitness abilities to build a solid foundation for success in any sport. If you ever have an opportunity to meet successful college or professional athletes, ask them what they did when they were 12 years old. Most likely they will say that they played outside everyday after school (developing fundamental fitness abilities) and competed on two or three different sport teams (developing a variety of sport-specific skills).

Our Program Philosophy

When developing plyometric programs for youth, it is important to remember that children and teenagers are not miniature adults. No matter how big, strong, or fast a child is, we must appreciate the fact that boys and girls are still growing and are often experiencing many activities for the very first time. Encourage—but do not force—boys and girls to try new activities and focus on learning new skills and having fun. Use words that are commensurate with each child's level of understanding and remind participants that it takes time to get in shape and learn a new skill.

The goals of our plyometric program are also different from adult programs. Enhancing the level of aerobic fitness and lowering blood pressure may be important motivating factors for adults, but boys and girls in plyometric programs just want to have fun, build friendships, and improve physical skills. Attempting to sell plyometric training to youth on the basis that it can enhance the quality of their lives is a losing proposition. In fact, since young children are concrete thinkers, they see little value in prolonged periods of monotonous exercise. While 30 minutes of continuous exercise on a stepping machine may be an enjoyable experience for some adults, most children (especially if they are sedentary and overweight) do not enjoy this type of activity and will probably drop out due to lack of interest and boredom. Watching children at a playground supports the premise that children habitually alternate movement with recovery—a natural process that should be encouraged and expected. Always respect children's feelings and appreciate the fact that the way they think and move is different from your own. Instead of asking youth to participate in an adult training program, modify exercises so children and teenagers can participate in a program that is designed for their own goals and expectations.

A major goal of our progressive plyometric program is for physical activity to become a habitual part of children's lives and hopefully persist into adulthood. With this objective in mind, we strive to maximize enjoyment and increase children's self-confidence in their own physical abilities. We resist the temptation to use the adult exercise paradigm and we get away from the "no pain, no gain" mentality. Youth programs that do nothing more than simply mimic adult programs fail to address the uniqueness of childhood and adolescence. We try to make every class or training session fun, interesting, and challenging, and we provide an opportunity for all children to feel good about their accomplishments. Instead of stressful competition in which most children fail, our progressive plyometric program focuses on positive experiences in which all kids succeed. Throughout childhood—and even throughout life—don't forget the importance of play, which is one of the ways in which we all learn. Getting kids excited about activities that are positive, non-threatening, and fun is what our progressive plyometric training program is all about.

At this point you hopefully have an understanding of how plyometrics work and how children and adolescents can benefit from this type of exercise. Nevertheless, it is not uncommon to have a few questions and concerns about this type of training. The following section addresses some of the most common questions from parents, physical educators, and youth coaches.

My daughter thinks exercise is boring. What can I do to get her moving? Boredom comes from monotony, not creative programming. Instead of prolonged periods of boring aerobic exercise, youth programs characterized by shorts bursts of physical activity interspersed with brief rest periods as needed are more fun for children and more consistent with how they naturally move. With enthusiastic leadership, challenging yet enjoyable exercises, and support from family and friends, children will learn that exercise can be fun and worthwhile.

The local youth coach thinks plyometrics are dangerous for kids. What should I do? An outdated view of plyometrics is that they are unsafe for children and teenagers. Since common playground activities such as jumping jacks and hopscotch are plyometric in nature, it is simply incorrect to think that plyometrics are dangerous. The key, however, is to introduce youth to this type of training with simple double-leg hops and then gradually progress to more challenging drills. While no evidence suggests that plyometrics are riskier that other sports and physical activities in which children regularly participate, a potential for injury does exist if the program is poorly designed and improperly progressed. You may want to educate this coach by telling him about our book!

How can I make plyometric training fun for kids? While many benefits are associated with plyometric training, it is important to remember that most boys and girls participate in physical activity programs to learn something new, make friends, and have fun. Therefore, it is important to listen to each child's concerns and design a program that is consistent with each child's needs and abilities. Be enthusiastic and provide an opportunity for all children to experience success and have an enjoyable experience.

Are plyometrics only for young athletes? No. Children and adolescents of all abilities can benefit from plyometric training. While plyometric training can be used to enhance athletic performance, regular participation in a plyometric program can enhance the fundamental fitness abilities of sedentary boys and girls too. At a time when a growing number of children and adolescents are regularly inactive, we believe that a progressive plyometric program can be particularly effective when sensibly incorporated into physical education classes and after-school recreation programs.

If my teenage daughter lifts weights at school why does she need to do plyometrics? While regular strength training offers numerous health and fitness benefits for youth, plyometric training is a unique form of exercise that is designed to mimic natural body positions and movement speeds that occur in daily life and sport. Plyometric training not only enhances muscular power, speed, and agility, but research suggests that regular plyometric training may reduce the risk of injury in youth sports, which may be particularly important for girls, who appear to suffer more sport-related knee injuries than boys.

Can kids perform plyometrics every day? Although plyometric exercises don't involve lifting barbells or dumbbells, they do involve moving one's body weight in a way that can place even greater demands on a child's developing musculoskeletal system. Therefore, the best results are seen when kids participate in a progressive plyometric training program twice per week on nonconsecutive days. Performing moderate- to high-intensity plyometric exercises every day will likely result in burnout, poor performance, and injury.

Isn't aerobic exercise an important part of a child's fitness program? Yes, aerobic exercise is important for cardiorespiratory health and fitness. However, this does not mean that children need to run or bike for 30 minutes without stopping. Since the natural activity habits of children are characterized by short bursts of activity interspersed with rest periods as needed, youth physical-activity programs that mimic the way children move are just as effective and a lot more fun.

At what age can my child start progressive plyometric training? When a child has the emotional maturity to accept and follow directions, then he is ready for our progressive plyometric program. In general, if children are ready for organized sports, then they are ready for participation in a structured conditioning program. As a point of reference, many seven- and eight-year-old boys and girls have successfully participated in our youth plyometric programs.

Summary

Although plyometrics were previously thought of as a method of conditioning elite adult athletes, a growing number of children and teenagers are now experiencing the benefits of plyometric training. In addition to enhancing muscle strength and bone strength, regular participation in a well-designed plyometric training program can better prepare young athletes for the demands of sports practice and competition. Moreover, plyometric training during childhood and adolescence may build the foundation for dramatic gains in muscular strength and power during adulthood. At a time when most children seem to be spending more time in front of the television than at the playground, the time is right to activate the lives of youth with our progressive plyometric training program.

Parents, teachers, and youth coaches should appreciate the potential benefits and concerns associated with this method of conditioning, and should realize that plyometrics are not a stand-alone exercise program. With appropriate guidance and progression, plyometrics can be a worthwhile additional to a fitness program that also includes other types of training. We need to use plyometrics sensibly to develop fundamental fitness skills while appreciating the uniqueness of children and teenagers. Our progressive plyometric program has proven to be a worthwhile and enjoyable experience for boys and girls, and we believe that our program can help spark an interest in regular physical activity.

2

Methods and Modes

Progressive Plyometrics Success Story

Sue was a gifted young soccer player who possessed tremendous balance and foot skills with the ball. However, she was not very strong and was significantly slower than her competition. Our progressive plyometric program helped Sue not only gain the strength and coordination she needed to excel in competitive soccer, but also helped her develop foot speed to match her soccer speed and her ability to read the game at a very high level.

Perhaps if our playgrounds were busier the issue of enhancing fundamental fitness abilities with plyometric training wouldn't be so pressing. But, unfortunately, physical education is sometimes viewed as an expendable part of the school curriculum and some American kids spend more time surfing the Internet than playing on the playground. In other countries such as Brazil, physical activity is still a part of children's daily lives. Brazilian kids walk to school, play outside for hours every day, and regularly participate in recreational activities such as soccer. Therefore, it is not surprising that the Brazilians dominate the sport of soccer on the international level. By developing fundamental fitness skills during childhood and adolescence, Brazilian soccer players are better prepared for the demands of sports practice and competition as adults.

Rather than focusing your efforts entirely on sport-specific training, redirect your efforts toward the development of fundamental fitness abilities. Boys and girls need to participate in a variety of locomotive (e.g., jumping), nonlocomotive (e.g., twisting), and manipulative (e.g., throwing) skills as part of play, games, recreation, physical education, and planned exercise sessions. By exposing boys and girls to different movements and technical skills, you not only help them develop proper body mechanics and improve their general athletic skills, but also increase their enthusiasm and willingness to participate in physical activities.

Figure 2-1. Even the youngest child enjoys the fun and movement of jumping.

While some youth who play sports are in great shape and can handle the stress from sports practice and competition without any additional training, most youth do not participate in regular physical activity. As simple as it sounds, these kids need to get in shape before they get in the game. In other words, forcing sedentary youth to participate in a highly competitive sports program that is too intense for their current abilities is a losing proposition. Not only will sedentary youth drop out of a vigorous sports-training program, but they will also lose confidence in their abilities to be physically active. Additionally, even young athletes who are in great shape will become better athletes if they enhance their strength, power, speed, and agility. While improving sports skills is important for enhancing the quality of sports practice and competition, improving a child's general athletic abilities will allow the child to use his sport-specific skills at a higher level of play.

The programs that we are presenting in this book are designed for children and teenagers, not adult athletes who are physically and psychologically more mature. It is important that we do not try to impose an adult training program on a child's body, as this could result in undesirable consequences for the development of the child. Since youth need to gradually increase the frequency and intensity of their exercise programs to avoid setbacks and injury, plyometric training should not be haphazardly programmed. Sedentary youth should begin with relatively easy, low-intensity plyometric exercises such as double-leg jumps to give their musculoskeletal system a chance to adapt to the new stress of regular exercise. When training athletes of any age, it is always better to undertrain than overtrain.

Starting an exercise program with simple activities provides youth with an opportunity to gain confidence in the exerciser's abilities to perform plyometrics. In some cases, youth may need to appreciate the fact that exercise training does not have to be painful to be beneficial. While many youth (and some parents) may be tempted to start with more advanced training programs, it is always better to start with less-intense exercises and gradually progress as children adapt to the new training stress and gain confidence to perform plyometrics correctly. All participants in our progressive plyometric training programs begin with simple jumps so that they have an opportunity to master the fundamentals of plyometric training before moving on to more advanced drills. While our workouts are challenging, they do provide an opportunity for participants to learn new skills before advancing to the next level.

Both art and science are included in designing plyometric training programs. The science is in understanding how plyometrics work and the art is in knowing which type of plyometric exercise a child is ready for at his stage of physical and mental development. Optimal training adaptations will take place when the demands of training are consistent with a child's stage of physical and mental development. For example, a 10-year-old girl who has been participating in a plyometric program for two years will be able to handle a more intense training program than a sedentary 14-year-old boy. Due to differences in body size and maturity, it is important to look beyond a child's chronological age when developing training program for children and teenagers.

It is important to keep in mind that the goal of our plyometric program is not limited to enhancing sports performance or reducing the likelihood of injury, but also includes teaching children about their bodies, promoting an interest in physical fitness, and having fun. Although the concept of having fun is easy to understand, it is more challenging to actually define the word "fun." We like to define fun as a balance between skill and challenge. If kids don't have the skills to perform a plyometric exercise, it probably won't be fun. And if an exercise is too challenging for a child, that won't be fun either. However, if a child has the skills to perform a drill (or believes he has the skills) and feels somewhat challenged by the task at hand, that's when exercise and progressive plyometrics become fun. Clearly, the art of developing plyometric programs involves understanding the abilities of each child so that the exercises are challenging while still being enjoyable.

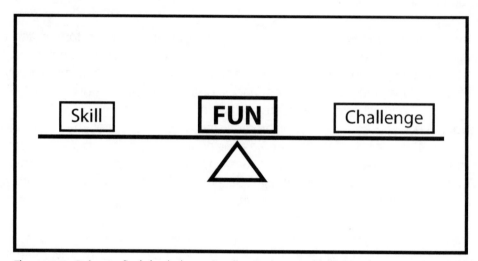

Figure 2-2. Strive to find the balance in all exercises and activities between the skills necessary and the amount of challenge present so that the kids have fun while they are exercising and playing.

When teaching youth plyometrics, we keep our verbal instructions short and use lots of demonstrations with constructive feedback. We want kids to focus on what to do rather than on what not to do. This is an important point to keep in mind because we are really trying to "teach" the neuromuscular system how to perform relatively complex movements more efficiently. This concept is known as motor learning and is especially important when teaching youth plyometric exercises. With quality practice sessions performed under the watchful eye of a knowledgeable coach, boys and girls can learn how to perform plyometrics correctly so they are better prepared for sports practice and competition. Since young athletes are often forced to train harder and longer to excel in sports, providing them with an opportunity to participate in a progressive plyometric program that prepares their bodies for the demands of sports practice and competition seems reasonable and worthwhile. That is why our plyometric program should begin several weeks before the sport season starts.

Current research studies suggest that youth who participate in a conditioning program that includes plyometric training for at least *six* weeks before the start of the season are better prepared for sports competition and less likely to suffer a sports-related injury. Chapter 4 presents the concepts of the program design for progressive plyometric exercise. In that chapter, we show you how to set up a plyometric conditioning program and how to sensibly progress training so that participants can maximize training adaptations with a minimal risk of injury.

A foundation built on strength, power, speed, and agility will prepare boys and girls for future sports success and lifelong physical activity. While aerobic exercise has become a dominant feature of some youth sport programs, prolonged periods of aerobic exercise are not needed for successful participation in most youth sports and, quite frankly, most boys and girls dislike prolonged periods of aerobic training. Furthermore, unlike adults, it seems that children have a more difficult time actually increasing their maximal aerobic capacity (i.e., VO_2 max) with training. Instead of running laps around the playing field, it simply makes sense for boys and girls to participate in activities that are worthwhile, effective, and fun.

Prior to every workout, we ask ourselves the following question: "What are we *really* trying to do with these kids?" The answer to this question does not involve winning a local championship, but rather sparking a lifelong interest in regular physical activity. We want boys and girls to take pleasure in fitness training and make physical activity a regular part of their lives.

Play Education

Two important areas of concern regarding the development of our progressive plyometric program are the quality of education and rate of progression. Parents and youth coaches should have an understanding of youth fitness guidelines and safety procedures, and should genuinely appreciate the uniqueness of childhood and adolescence. While enhancing the level of cardiorespiratory fitness may be an important motivating factor for adults, most kids just want to have fun, build friendships, and feel good about their accomplishments. Selling our plyometric program to children by spouting the potential health benefits of physical activity simply won't work. On the other hand, when kids see other kids experiencing success and having fun they are more likely to try it. Although positive feedback from an adult can be meaningful, nothing beats one child telling another that "this is fun!"

Figure 2-3. When youth enjoy the exercise, game, or sport they are playing, they will let you know! Always strive to keep exercise fun for the kids.

While children should be made aware of the potential health benefits of plyometric training (e.g., stronger bones and reduced risk of sports injuries), do not overlook the real reasons most children engage in regular physical activity. Sometimes it is helpful for parents and youth coaches to remember what they were like as children to get a healthy perspective. Have you ever seen a child running for 30 minutes at a playground without stopping? Probably not. Recognize the fact that children are active in different ways than adults. Take the time to carefully manipulate the intensity of the games and activities to mimic the natural activity patterns of youth.

Boys and girls should be provided with an opportunity to participate in a plyometric training program under the watchful eye of a caring and knowledgeable instructor, coach, or parent who understands and genuinely appreciates the need for age-appropriate instruction, sensible progression, and program safety. It is important that adults who are supervising young athletes have a solid understanding of plyometric training because if youth practice plyometrics incorrectly they will only get better at performing plyometrics incorrectly. Although making a mistake is part of the learning process, without proper guidance and instruction kids can actually get comfortable performing plyometrics the wrong way. Remember "show and tell" from primary school? We follow a similar teaching strategy when working with youth. After positioning the participants so they can all have a good view of the teacher or coach, try the following strategy when introducing a new skill to the group:

Step 1: *Name* the skill. Use one name and stick with it to avoid confusion in the future.

Step 2: *Explain* the skill. Use simple terms to describe the drill and keep explanations short. Tell kids how the drill can help them.

Step 3: *Show* the skill. The most important part is for kids to see how to perform the drill correctly. Show the skill several times and from different angles so all participants can see a full picture of it.

Step 4: *Perform* the skill. Ask the kids to perform the drill and offer guidance on proper body position and jumping mechanics. Positive, constructive feedback not only helps kids perform the skill correctly, but also serves to motivate kids to practice.

You need to make sure that boys and girls learn how to perform plyometrics the right way the first time, and you also need to know how to correct errors when children make them. Beginners need to learn how to perform plyometrics right from the start so that incorrect movement patterns are not repeated, and coaches need to teach plyometric exercises properly so that they do not reinforce improper techniques.

Plyometric training should also be consistent with each child's needs and abilities. A major concern we have with many plyometric training programs is that they are too advanced for kids. Adult exercise guidelines and training philosophies should not be imposed on boys and girls who are physically and psychologically less mature. Too often the frequency and intensity of adult plyometric training programs exceed a child's abilities and the recovery periods are inadequate for a child's fitness level. For this reason, it is extremely important to gradually progress from simple to more complex drills. Most kids have never participated in an organized, progressive plyometric training program before, and they don't know what plyometric training feels like. If they perform

Figure 2-4. We always stress proper form to our young athletes, and encourage coaches and parents to never sacrifice proper technique to complete a certain number of repetitions.

endless repetitions of any exercises they will get bored with the training program, develop incorrect technique. and increase their risk of injury. In our programs, children perform plyometric exercises twice per week and we focus on the quality of the movement instead of the quantity. We have kids think about every repetition as they jump, hop, or skip. Once movement speed or technique begins to falter, we stop the exercise and take a short rest. While errors are a part of learning, repeating the same error over and over again will slow down the learning process.

Plan for Success

Over the past two decades we have learned a lot about designing plyometric training programs. Sport scientists have explored the effects of different types of training on a variety of performance measures and have provided us with general recommendations for achieving specific goals, reducing boredom, and avoiding overtraining. While many variables need to be considered when designing a plyometric training program, one program design factor that has become obvious to the sport scientist is the need for program variation. A popular term for periodically varying training variables to promote long-term gains and avoid boredom and overtraining is *periodization*.

The underlying concept of periodization is based on the General Adaptation Syndrome, which proposes that after a period of time adaptations to a new training program will no longer take place and "staleness" may result. This does not mean that every plyometric workout needs to be more intense or more voluminous (i.e., more sets and repetitions) than the previous session, but rather that as the child adapts to the training stimulus, the demands need to become more challenging over time to maintain their effectiveness. This challenge can be met by increasing the intensity of the exercises, increasing the number of exercises, or simply by changing the choice of exercises. By periodically varying the training program, performance gains will be optimized and boredom will be reduced. The concept of periodization is particularly important for youth, who tend to get bored, lose interest, and drop out if they perform the same exercise program over and over again.

While no single model of periodization exists, the general concept is to prioritize training goals and then develop a long-term plan that varies throughout the training period. Our progressive plyometric program consists of three levels, which we call the bronze, silver, and gold programs. Each level represents a progression sequence of exercises in which the participants progress to the next stage only after understanding and mastering the technical requirements of the previous level. In our plyometric program, boys and girls progress from the bronze to the silver and eventually the gold program as they master simple exercises and gain confidence in their abilities to perform more complex drills.

As children progress to the silver and gold levels, we purposefully reduce the number of sets from two to one during the first week of training at each level due to the intensity of the new exercises. As children progress from the bronze to the silver and eventually the gold program we also reduce the number of repetitions from 10 to eight and finally to six, respectively. While we value the importance of program variation and progression, we also understand that the rate of performance gains depends upon the manner in which the program is progressed (Figure 2-5). Hurrying the progression of any youth fitness program can result in undesirable consequences such as poor performances, burnout, or injury.

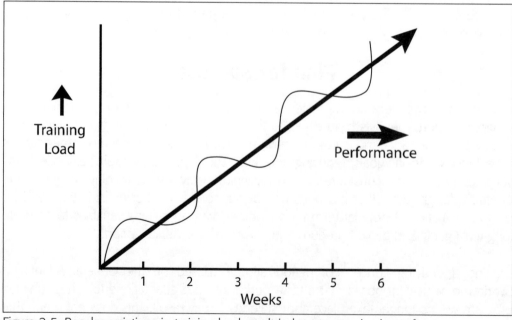

Figure 2-5. Regular variations in training load result in long-term gains in performance.

Due to the physical stress of plyometric training, some parents and youth coaches may need to consider the total exercise picture because some aspiring young athletes may need to decrease the time they spend practicing sport skills to allow time for progressive plyometric training. In other words, plyometric exercises should not simply be added onto a young athlete's daily routine without considering each individual's current schedule, which may already include several hours of physical activity from sport training, physical education, or a part-time job that involves manual labor. While there is nothing wrong with training hard on your hard days, we believe that it is just as important to plan for adequate rest and recovery on your easy days.

Training Modes

Unlike most fitness programs that require expensive equipment, activities in our plyometric program require only inexpensive gym supplies, creativity, and energy. We developed this broad-based exercise program with the goal of reaching as many boys and girls as possible. We use cones, medicine balls, and body weight exercises to keep our program challenging and fun. By using one's own body weight and simple equipment, an almost infinite number of exercises can be created to achieve specific training goals. While we value strength-building exercise with barbells, dumbbells, and appropriate weight machines, all the exercises in our program can be completed with minimal expense. Our plyometric exercises are designed to mimic natural body positions and movement speeds that occur in daily life and game situations.

Although it may require a longer period of time to master proper technique on a plyometric exercise compared to a single-joint weight machine exercise such as a leg extension, plyometrics require greater balance and coordination, which is what makes this type of training so beneficial for children and teenagers. Moreover, proper fit is not an issue when using one's body weight because "one size fits all."

Although exercises that train individual muscles or muscle groups can be effective, we prefer exercises that train the body to function as a unit instead of separate parts. Boys and girls need more than strong muscles; they need to develop athletic qualities that enhance movement competence. We believe the best piece of training equipment is one's own body. Body weight exercises are challenging and require the use of stabilizing and assisting muscles to maintain the correct body position while performing an exercise correctly. In addition, body weight exercises that require agility, speed, and balance require kids to think about what they are doing and how they are moving. This type of training is cognitively stimulating and can result in real learning through task-oriented approaches that enable each child to learn the best way to perform a drill or activity correctly.

In addition to body weight exercises, we also use medicine balls to challenge and excite children in our program. Medicine balls are weighted vinyl, polyurethane, or leather balls that are portable, easy to carry, and available in a variety of colors, weights, and sizes (from the size of a baseball to the size of a basketball). Some medicine balls have a textured surface for easy gripping, and others are inflatable and bounce. We have found that medicine ball training can be a challenging, motivating, and fun method of conditioning for boys and girls of all ages and abilities.

Figure 2-6. Using a medicine ball is a safe and easy way to not only gradually increase the difficulty of an exercise, but also to increase the "fun factor" of performing a particular movement.

Although some medicine balls weigh more than 15 pounds, children in our plyometric programs start with two-pound balls and gradually progress to four- to six-pound balls as strength and exercise technique improve. Obviously, it is desirable to have medicine balls of different shapes and sizes to accommodate the needs and abilities of all youth in your program. We use color-coded medicine balls in our program so the coaches and participants can easily keep track of the loads that are being used. Commercially made medicine balls are relatively inexpensive (about $15 to $40, depending on weight and material) and are available from most sporting good companies or online fitness equipment distributors.

Summary

While the need for children and teenagers to participate in progressive plyometric training may seem minimal to some parents and youth coaches, it is important to remember that participation in physical activity should not begin with competitive sport but should evolve out of preparatory conditioning. With qualified instruction, sensible progression, and a focus on having fun, boys and girls of all abilities can benefit from participation in our progressive plyometric training program. Instead of expensive gym equipment, all you need are a few simple supplies and an understanding of program-design considerations. It is clear that we have an opportunity to enhance the health and fitness of boys and girls by encouraging them to participate in a developmentally appropriate plyometric training program. In the following chapters, we provide you with all the information and tools you need to implement our bronze, silver ,and gold plyometric training programs.

3

Training for Success

Progressive Plyometrics Success Story

Patrick joined our after-school plyometric program after his parents heard about our approach to developing "athleticism" in all youth. Although Patrick was not a "gifted" athlete, after completing our program he enhanced his fundamental fitness abilities and gained confidence in his ability to be physically active. Patrick continues to participate regularly in our after-school program and recently joined a baseball team.

Plyometric training can be one of the most potent, efficient, and effective methods of conditioning for children and adolescents, provided that the program is carefully designed and qualified instruction is available. While there is no minimum age for participating in our plyometric training program, boys and girls should have the emotional maturity to accept and follow directions and should appreciate the benefits and concerns associated with this method of training. In our youth programs, success is not defined by the number of championship rings, but rather by the willingness of each child to work hard, try their best, and develop healthy habits that can last a lifetime. Realizing that only a very small percentage of the young athletes we coach will ever reach the professional ranks, our primary goal is to provide a positive experience for all boys and girls in our youth fitness programs.

In general, if a child is ready for participation in some type of sport activity then he may be ready for our progressive plyometric training program. Look at the movement patterns and skills on any playground, and you will see children as young as two to three years of age performing plyometric movements. As a point of reference, seven- and eight-year-old children have participated in our structured youth programs over the years and most of them continue to lead active lives as teenagers and adults. Although a preparticipation medical examination is not mandatory for apparently healthy boys and girls, we suggest that youth with known or suspected health problems such as asthma, diabetes, or recent surgery see their doctor before participating in this or any other any exercise program.

Train Smart

While no evidence indicates that plyometric training is "riskier" than other sports and activities in which youth regularly participate, plyometric training is a specialized method of conditioning that requires appropriate overload, gradual progression, and adequate recovery between exercise sessions. Moreover, plyometric programs should include proper coaching, a safe training environment, and a slow but steady advancement from education to progression to function. Since the performance of a plyometric exercise is a learned skill, proper instruction is needed to ensure continuation of correct exercise technique. As you will see, boys and girls of all abilities can participate in our program with very little equipment and can complete a workout in about 30 minutes. However, for our progressive plyometric training program to be most effective, coaches and participants must adhere to our program guidelines and believe in our training philosophy.

In our progressive plyometric program, we have adapted the process of learning plyometrics to meet the physical and psychosocial needs of children and teenagers.

> • Qualified adults should provide instruction and supervision
> • Begin with basic drills and gradually progress
> • Focus on the quality of movement, not the quantity
> • Perform warm-up activities prior to every exercise session
> • Allow adequate time for rest and recovery between hard workout sessions
> • Vary the training program to optimize adaptations and reduce boredom

Figure 3-1. General youth activity guidelines

Our program gradually exposes youth to increasingly more complex drills and provides an opportunity for all participants to feel successful. Unlike a rigid training regimen characterized by a "no pain, no gain" mentality, our program progresses the child through a menu of strength, balance, agility, and plyometric drills that are consistent with a child's level of physical and mental maturity. As you become familiar with our methods and modes of training, you will see how our progressive plyometric program can replace the makeshift conditioning programs than are too complex, too long, or simply unsafe. Our approach is different. Instead of a two-hour workout that leaves kids feeling worn-out and tired, our 30-minute training sessions include carefully chosen exercises that have a distinct purpose. The quality of our program, not the quantity, is what makes our program unique. In fact, the design of our youth workouts may surprise you because our program can be incorporated into sports practices, physical education classes, or after-school recreational programs.

In addition to understanding and appreciating the needs and abilities of the participants in your program, it is essential to adhere to fundamental training principles. We refer to the fundamental principles of plyometric training as the P.R.O.S., which stands for, **P**rogression, **R**ecovery, **O**verload, and **S**pecificity.

Progression

A fundamental tenet of exercise training is the principle of progression. This age-old principle refers to the fact that the demands placed on the body must be progressively increased over time to make continual gains. This includes, but is not limited to, performing more repetitions, using a heavier weight, and performing more complex exercises. As muscles become stronger and more powerful, they will adapt to the exercise program. If the program doesn't change the muscles won't change. According to the principle of progression, the training program must be advanced at a rate that is compatible with the abilities of each child to make long-term gains in strength and power.

Once youth have mastered the proper execution of a drill, they are more likely to direct their efforts toward maximal force development, which is the goal of plyometric training. This is where the art and science of developing plyometric programs come into play. If the training program does not progress, it will become stale and adaptations will no longer take place. Conversely, if the training program exceeds a child's capabilities the risk of injury will increase and the enjoyment of the training experience will diminish.

A common mistake in designing a youth plyometric training program is to recommend too many sets and repetitions of too many exercises. A plyometric exercise should not be so difficult that a child cannot react quickly and perform each repetition explosively with proper exercise form. The key to keep in mind is to minimize contact time with the ground while maintaining proper body mechanics. Thus, the training frequency, intensity, volume, and progression need to be carefully programmed. Proper progression and planning of a plyometric training program will optimize gains, prevent boredom, and reduce the stress from overtraining. Our progressive program is designed to gradually progress the child through strength, plyometric, speed, and agility exercises. Since most youth have no experience performing plyometric exercises, we recommend that all boys and girls—regardless of athletic ability—begin at the bronze level. Over time they can progress to the silver level and eventually to the gold level to maximize adaptations to the training program.

Recovery

It is noteworthy that the progressive plyometric training programs that are the most beneficial for youth have a training frequency, on average, of two nonconsecutive days per week. While too many days between workouts can initiate the detraining process, a downfall of many youth plyometric programs is lack of enough recovery between workouts. We call this *underrecovery*. A reduction in athletic performance and an increased risk of injury can result from poor programming characterized by frequent training sessions and inadequate rest and recovery. Even though aspiring young athletes who participate in carefully designed plyometric programs can perform advanced plyometric drills, the key is not to overdose kids with frequent periods of high-intensity and high-volume training sessions. It takes time to learn how to perform high-intensity drills properly with maximum effort.

Although the amount of recovery needed between plyometric workouts may vary depending upon the intensity of the training program and individual abilities, allowing at least 48 to 72 hours between plyometric workouts will accelerate the adaptations to the training program and therefore reduce a child's injury potential. However, a training frequency recommendation of two to three days per week assumes that no competition days or other intense practice sessions take place during the week. If other intense bouts of exercise are scheduled, then the plyometric training frequency should be reduced. Since delayed onset muscle soreness can result from plyometric training, one day of rest between workout sessions may not be adequate for all participants. In fact, since children and teenagers are still growing and developing, they may actually need more time for rest and recovery between plyometric workouts than adults. Rest may be particularly important for competitive young athletes who may be less willing to reduce the intensity and/or volume of their training program and may therefore need additional guidance and counseling from their coach, teacher, or parent.

While it is tempting to focus only on program design variables such as sets, repetitions, and exercise choice, it is important for parents and youth coaches to realize that what is done *between* exercise sessions can have a significant impact on what is done *during* exercise sessions. During a plyometric workout, the stress from jumping, hopping, and throwing actually results in a breakdown of some muscle tissue. The desired adaptations to plyometric training take place on the "off day," or recovery day, when the body has the opportunity to recover from the physical stress of plyometric training. When sensibly programmed and monitored, plyometric training can offer numerous health and fitness benefits. Remember that the "more is better" attitude is not only counterproductive, but also will likely result in injury, burnout, or poor performance.

Figure 3-2. All children should be encouraged to stay hydrated by drinking water before, during, and after every workout.

Well-planned activities and recovery strategies are needed to maximize adaptation and return to an optimal performance state. Due to the high levels of physical stress involved with plyometric training, the planning of lower level, active rest activities and actual passive recovery need to be implemented in the overall training program to allow for a maximal level of recovery so that performance of each exercise can be done at an optimal level. With a systematic use of some or all of the methods described in Figure 3-3, participants will likely recover faster from the stress of plyometric training. Coaches, teachers, and parents should talk about the potential value of different recovery strategies and should realize that a recovery strategy works best for one child may not be effective for another.

- Cool down: Finish each workout with a cool-down including walking and static stretching.
- Stay hydrated: Replenish body fluids and electrolytes by drinking water, juice, sports drinks, and other caffeine-free beverages throughout the day, even when you're not thirsty. Stay hydrated during the workout by drinking cool water every 15 to 20 minutes.
- Fuel up: Consume a food-snack or beverage containing carbohydrates and protein within one hour of finishing every workout. This will quickly replenish energy stores.
- Get adequate sleep: Most kids need about eight to nine hours of sleep per night and young athletes may need more than that.
- Vary workouts. Make workouts more fun and effective by periodically changing the training program.
- Allow time for recovery: Since training adaptations take place during the recovery period, allow time for adequate recovery and rejuvenation between training sessions.

Figure 3-3. Recovery strategies for youth

Overload

The overload principle states that the body must be exercised at a level beyond that to which it is presently accustomed. Since most kids have had little or no formal experience participating in a structured plyometric program, it makes sense to begin plyometric training at the bronze level with low-intensity hops, skips, and throws. Starting slowly will give the musculoskeletal systems of boys and girls a chance to adapt to the training stress. Furthermore, performance adaptations resulting from more intense plyometric training during the first few weeks will not offer any additional benefit and may even be injurious. As training progresses the window of adaptation begins to shrink and more advanced plyometric exercises are needed to make continual gains. In other words, training programs that were effective during the first few weeks of training may become ineffective after the initial adaptation period. As you can see, the principles of overload and progression are closely related.

Specificity

The principle of training specificity is one of the more important factors to keep in mind when designing training programs, because the adaptations that occur in the body in response to a training program are as simple or as complex as the training program itself. Training adaptations are specific to the muscle groups involved in the exercise, the type of muscle action, the movement pattern, and the velocity of contraction. Consequently, the more closely an exercise mimics a specific sport action, the greater the carryover of strength and power to that sport action. Although few, if any, training activities have 100% carryover to a sport or activity in terms of specificity, conditioning programs that include types of training (e.g., plyometrics) that are specific to the sport may be most effective for enhancing sports performance.

Just think about a child jumping for a rebound in basketball or quickly moving to get to the ball during a soccer game. Since plyometric exercises such as single-leg hops and lateral jumps link strength with speed of movement, they are more likely to result in desirable changes in athletic performance than other methods of training. Proper planning is essential, so think about which movements (e.g., vertical jump, linear jump, and change of direction) a child needs to develop for a particular sport prior to developing a training program. Because nearly all sports involve sprinting, jumping, throwing, or changing directions, our progressive plyometric program uses all of these movements, thereby providing youth with the fundamental fitness skills and movements that will help them to be successful in any sport or movement activity.

Although traditional strength-training exercises such as the leg extension will enhance a child's muscular strength, multijoint exercises performed at higher velocities are preferable for optimal gains in jumping or sprinting ability. Unlike exercises performed slowly on weight machines, plyometric exercises are dynamic movements that can duplicate joint velocity and angular movements consistent with sport activities. This does not mean that every exercise needs to be performed at a high velocity, but rather that over time the general stress or overload placed upon a child's musculoskeletal system must begin to match the physical characteristics of the sport

Figure 3-4. Most sport skills involve some component of plyometric exercise. Training even the youngest athlete in the proper techniques of progressive plyometric exercise will yield better results.

activity itself. Plyometrics teach the body how to react more quickly by emphasizing quick ground movements and explosive upper-body muscle actions. In our youth programs, we integrate slow-velocity strength-building exercises with high-velocity plyometric drills to develop proper movement patterns and optimize training adaptations.

For example, a young basketball player who wants to improve her jumping ability would benefit from exercises such as body weight squats and standing jumps. Once she has mastered these double-leg drills she can advance to more challenging exercises such as single-leg dips and single-leg hops that are very specific to basketball. Even though this young athlete may want to play her sport to get into shape, it is unlikely that she will make the greatest gains in jumping ability without participating in a multifaceted conditioning program. The bottom line is that enhancing fitness skills will enable an athlete to perform sports skills on the court or playing field at a higher level.

Program Variables

Plyometrics are not a magical form of exercise. However, they can be a uniquely valuable form of training if sensibly incorporated into a well-designed conditioning program. While the general design of a plyometric workout is similar to other types of exercise such as strength training, the following seven program variables should be considered when designing a plyometric training program—the choice of exercise, order of exercise, training intensity, training tempo, number of sets, rest periods between sets and exercises, and training frequency.

Choice of Exercise

A limitless number of plyometric exercises can be used to enhance muscle function and performance. In fact, any explosive movement that involves jumping, hopping, skipping, throwing, or sprinting can be considered plyometric. Since it is important to select exercises that are appropriate for an individual's fitness level and training goals, it is important to group exercises as low intensity (e.g., double-leg hop), moderate intensity (e.g., lateral cone hop), or high intensity (e.g., drop jump).

Order of Exercise

Plyometric exercises should be performed early in the workout, when the body is fresh and capable of performing exercises with energy and vigor. If plyometrics are performed at the end of a workout, the neuromuscular system will be fatigued and the child will not experience the greatest benefit from plyometric training. In our program, participants perform plyometrics after our warm-up activities and several body weight strength-building movements. The strength-building exercises not only "prime" the neuromuscular system for the demands of plyometric training, but they also provide a needed opportunity for boys and girls to practice proper form and technique on a variety of important movement skills such as the squat. This type of pre-event protocol is sometimes called movement preparation and we believe that it is an essential component of our youth training programs. The key, however, is to excite the neuromuscular system without undue fatigue. If the movement preparation period is too long or if the exercises are too intense, performance on the plyometric drills will be suboptimal and training adaptations will be less than expected. Remember, plyometrics are not designed to be a stand-alone exercise program.

Training Intensity

The most important variable in the design of a workout is the training intensity. Gains in muscle performance are influenced by the intensity of the training session in relation to the number of repetitions performed. We have participants perform between six and 10 repetitions of each exercise. While our strength-building exercises are performed in a controlled manner, each repetition of a plyometric exercise is performed quickly and explosively. Regardless of movement speed, we always focus on the quality of the movement as opposed to the quantity of training repetitions. From our experiences, technique and movement speed begin to wane after 10 repetitions.

Training Tempo

According to the principle of specificity, the tempo at which an exercise is performed will affect the adaptations that take place. For example, fast tempo plyometric training is more likely to enhance muscular power than slower tempo strength training. While strength-building exercises should be performed at a slow to moderate tempo, plyometric drills should be performed at a fast tempo provided that *every* repetition is a quality movement. When this is accomplished, optimal gains in performance will be realized. Since the performance of different training tempos within a workout may provide variety and progression within a workout, our youth program includes *both* slow to moderate tempo strength exercises, and faster tempo plyometric and agility training.

Training Sets

A set refers to a group of repetitions performed continuously. While there is much debate regarding the number of sets that should be performed per exercise, it should be noted that not every exercise needs to be performed for the same number of sets. When designing a plyometric training program for beginners, it is reasonable to begin with a program that consists of only a single set of repetitions and then gradually increase the number of sets and repetitions depending on personal goals and time available for training. Different combinations of sets and exercises are not only effective and time-efficient, but they also allow for variation in the training stimulus, which may be vital for long-term gains. In our program, boys and girls perform one to two sets of a variety of exercises.

Rest Periods

The length of the rest period between sets and exercises is an important, but often overlooked, training variable. In general, the length of the rest period will influence energy recovery and the adaptations that take place. When performing plyometric exercises, longer rest periods are needed to maximize muscle performance. In the training of adult athletes, the use of long rest periods (about two to three minutes) is critical so that the athlete can complete each repetition of every exercise with maximal intensity. However, we are not dealing with adult athletes here, but rather with children and teenagers who have shorter attention spans. Prolonged rest periods between sets and exercises often result in boredom and horseplay among young participants. It is in this situation that the science of plyometric training needs to be carefully balanced with the art of developing youth plyometric programs.

We recommend beginning with shorter rest intervals between sets and exercises to keep kids focused. If you notice that performance begins to wane on the second set, alter the training program and lengthen the rest periods between sets. While research with adults would suggest rest intervals up to three minutes between sets and exercises, our coaching observation suggests that most boys and girls, even the elite young athlete, will get bored with a rest interval of much longer than one to two minutes.

Therefore, since the rest interval is dependant upon the intensity of training, it is our recommendation to use a rest interval of about 30 seconds for the bronze level, 60 seconds for the silver level, and 90 seconds for the gold level. If the kids need more time, prolong the rest period and ask them to walk to aid in the recovery process. Participants should have enough time to perform at a maximum intensity without letting the muscles cool down.

Note that we do not recommend very short rest periods (less than 30 seconds) due to the discomfort and high blood lactate concentrations that result from this type of training. This is an important point to keep in mind when teaching plyometrics to participants of any fitness level. Fatigue interferes with the performance of any drill and can impede the learning process. This will result in a decrease in performance and children will mostly likely feel frustrated because they will not be able to achieve their expected level of speed, distance, or height. A true plyometric exercise requires a brief period of vigorous exercise followed by an active recovery period of walking that prepares the body for the next set of drills.

Training Frequency

Training frequency refers to the number of training sessions per week. While low-intensity plyometric drills may be performed more frequently than high-intensity plyometric drills, the need for recovery between any two plyometric training sessions should not be underestimated. The key point is that training adaptations occur during the recovery period, not during the training session. Since children and adolescents may need more time for recovery between workouts than adults, we suggest a plyometric training frequency of twice per week on nonconsecutive days.

However, during a competitive sports season, a training frequency of twice per week may be too much for some young athletes. Difficulty recovering from a workout, muscle soreness that lasts more than two days, discomfort in the joints, and a lack of motivation to exercise are a few signs and symptoms that are characteristic of overtraining, which can eventually result in a decrease in performance and injury. The bottom line is that plyometrics should not simply be added onto an athlete's training schedule, but rather sensibly incorporated into a periodized training program. In some cases, young athletes may need to decrease the amount of time they spend practicing sport skills to allow for preparatory training that includes plyometrics. Therefore, the frequency of training needs to be consistent with individual needs, abilities, and concurrent sport activities.

Planning a Workout

Although an endless number of exercises can be performed, we have found that the following format works best for our youth programs. Each training session includes a five- to 10-minute dynamic warm-up period, 20 to 30 minutes of conditioning activities (including strength, plyometric, and speed drills), and about five minutes of cool-down activities. We explain, demonstrate, then have the participants perform each exercise while we watch and provide constructive feedback. This approach has proven highly effective for eliciting enthusiastic and energetic responses from children and teenagers.

Part 1: Dynamic Warm-up

Despite the universal practice of pre-event static stretching, little evidence exists that static stretching has a favorable impact on muscle performance or injury rates in children and teenagers. On the other hand, pre-event dynamic warm-up activities that are designed to elevate body temperature, excite the neuromuscular system, and maximize active ranges of motion have been shown to positively influence muscle performance in children and teenagers. In addition, since a variety of movement skills can be practiced during the warm-up, participants have another opportunity to practice

Figure 3-5. We recommend a dynamic warm-up to prepare the kids for plyometric exercise. Dynamic warm-ups are a safe and effective way to prepare the muscles and the body for the demands of any exercise.

fundamental movement skills. Our warm-up protocol consists of a three-minute "easy" jog followed by several dynamic exercises that prepare the body for the upcoming workout. Each dynamic movement is performed for about six to 10 repetitions and repeated twice with a brief (five- to 10-second) recovery period between sets. For a little variety, you can create a warm-up using cones, hula-hoops, agility ladders, or whatever else is available. When participants feel warm, they start to sweat and are ready to begin the conditioning phase of the workout.

Sample Dynamic Warm-up Drills

High Knee Lift. While standing in place, lift your right knee toward your chest, raise the body up on the toes of the left foot, and touch your right ankle with both hands. Repeat on the other side (Figure 3-6).

Figure 3-6. High knee lift

Standing Flutter. While standing in place with both arms extended overhead, extend your right arm and left leg backward several inches and then return to the starting position. Repeat with the opposite limbs (Figure 3-7).

Figure 3-7. Standing flutter

Toes In and Out. While standing in place, first march your feet to turn the toes out and the heels in, and then turn the toes in and heels out (Figure 3-8).

Figure 3-8. Toes in and out

Torso Twists. Stand with your hands clasped behind your head. While looking forward and keeping the upper body facing forward, start marching in place and turn the hips 90 degrees to the right. Then, turn to the left as far as possible, focusing on trunk rotation (Figure 3-9).

Figure 3-9. Torso twists

Lateral Shuffle. Lower your body into a half-squat position and take five steps to the right. Pause briefly before taking five steps to the left to return to the starting position (Figure 3-10).

Figure 3-10. Lateral shuffle

Giant Steps. From a standing position, take a long step forward with your right leg and then bring the left foot forward as far as possible. Repeat for the desired number of repetitions. Then, step backward as far as possible, alternating right and left feet. Note that this exercise works on balance as well as serving as a good warm-up exercise (Figure 3-11).

Figure 3-11. Giant steps

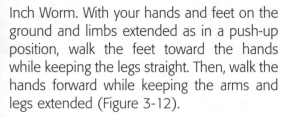

Inch Worm. With your hands and feet on the ground and limbs extended as in a push-up position, walk the feet toward the hands while keeping the legs straight. Then, walk the hands forward while keeping the arms and legs extended (Figure 3-12).

Figure 3-12. Inch worm

Part 2: Conditioning Activities

The conditioning activities in this section are designed to improve general athletic qualities and enhance movement efficiency. The exercises should be performed in the order that they are listed because each movement has a distinct purpose. Our conditioning workout progresses from slow and simple to fast and complex. As we have discussed throughout this text, it is the quality of each movement, not the quantity, that is critical for any type of movement training.

	Bronze Exercises		Silver Exercises		Gold Exercises	
Week	1	2	3	4	5	6
Set(s)	1	2	1	2	1	2
Repetitions	10	10	8	8	6	6

Figure 3-13. Summary of sets and repetitions

Strength Exercises

Following the warm-up period, participants perform several body weight strength-building exercises. Strength exercises provide participants with an opportunity to enhance their muscular strength while developing sound movement skills on selected upper- and lower-body exercises. The idea is to first perform the movement at a controlled speed before attempting to perform the drill explosively. In our program, participants perform one or two sets of six to 10 repetitions of three strength-building exercises.

Plyometric Exercises

After the muscles are warmed-up and the neuromuscular system is 'turned on," it is time to teach the muscles how to function at a higher level. This phase of the training session includes plyometric exercises that are specifically designed to enhance muscular power. Following a review of proper training procedures, we demonstrate the correct technique and offer positive and constructive comments. Since the key is to overload the neuromuscular system without undue fatigue, we begin with low-intensity activities that are moderately challenging so children can develop fundamental skills and gain confidence in their abilities prior to progressing to more advanced exercises. Whenever possible, we like to introduce new drills based on exercises that the kids already know because children will learn more quickly when they are somewhat familiar with the drills they are learning. When children are able to perform an exercise correctly, the movement becomes easier. Participants perform one or two sets of six to 10 repetitions of 10 plyometric exercises.

Although plyometric training can certainly raise an individual's exercise heart rate into the target heart rate zone (e.g., 70 to 85% of predicted maximal heart rate), our plyometric programs typically result in more of an interval type of conditioning characterized by increases and decreases in exercise heart rates during the training session (Figure 3-14). While the average heart rate for the 12-year-old boy in Figure 3-2 was about 150 beats per minute, his heart rate seemed to wax and wane between 140 and 180 for the entire workout. This is similar to the heart rate response during sport activities in which movement is typically characterized by haphazard increases and decreases in exercise intensity.

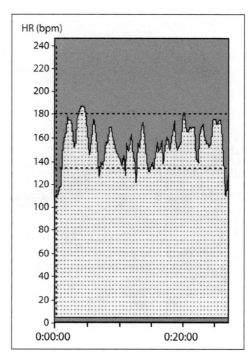

Figure 3-14. Progressive plyometric training will generally result in a heart rate response that is consistent with moderate to vigorous physical activity.

Speed and Agility Training

The last section of our conditioning program includes exercises designed to enhance speed and agility. We like to think of these drills as plyometrics in action because this is where we put it all together. Since this type of training requires a high degree of skill, each activity should be short (less than 10 seconds) so that fatigue does not become a factor. These activities are specifically designed to enhance a child's ability to accelerate, decelerate, change direction, and then accelerate again. Participants perform only one or two sets of each drill. Since a tired body cannot perform these drills with energy and vigor, it is important to allow for adequate recovery between each speed and agility drill.

Part 3: Warm-Down Activities

During the warm-down period, which is sometimes called the cool-down period, we decrease the intensity of the training session and encourage children to walk for about three minutes at a comfortable pace. Participants then perform several static stretches for the upper and lower body. We ask the participants to hold each stretch for about 15 to 30 seconds and repeat two or three times. During the warm-down we reflect on what the children learned to help us plan future workouts. Even though tangible outcome measures (e.g., increasing vertical jump) are important, when working with children it is important to focus on intrinsic factors such as skill improvement, personal success, and having fun. If our plyometric conditioning program is performed before physical education class or a sports practice, then the following static stretching exercises should be performed at the end of class or practice.

Warm-down Static Stretching Exercises

Chest Stretch. Place both hands behind your head with your elbows bent. Slowly move the elbows backward while keeping your hands clasped on your head (Figure 3-15).

Figure 3-15. Chest stretch

Modified Hurdler's Stretch. In a seated position with one leg straight, place your other leg on the inside of the straight leg and reach forward (Figure 3-16).

Figure 3-16. Modified hurdler's stretch

Butterfly Stretch. In a seated position with an erect spine, touch the soles of your feet together, bend the knees and allow them to drop (Figure 3-17).

Figure 3-17. Butterfly stretch

Quadriceps Stretch. Lying on your side with your body straight, bend the top knee and bring the heel toward your buttocks while holding the foot with one hand. Then, push your hips forward (Figure 3-18).

Figure 3-18. Quadriceps stretch

Press-Up Low-Back Stretch. Lying on your stomach, put your hands in front of your shoulders and then press up until your arms are extended while trying to keep the hips in contact with the ground (Figure 3-19).

Figure 3-19. Press-up low-back stretch

Calf Stretch. In a standing position with your feet staggered about two or three feet from a wall, lean against the wall with both hands, trying to keep the back leg straight and the front leg slightly bent (Figure 3-20).

Figure 3-20. Calf stretch

Workout Advice

A youth conditioning program can help children and adolescents reach their performance goals, provided that the program is properly developed, organized, and progressed. To help boys and girls get the most from their workouts, consider the following recommendations.

Provide a Safe Environment. Qualified adults should provide close supervision and be prepared to deal with any emergencies. Adults should have access to first aid equipment and know when to call 911. Adults should remove any potential hazards from the activity area and, if necessary, know when to modify an exercise or activity to make it safer. All participants should wear sneakers (with laces tied) and plyometrics should ideally be performed on a yielding landing surface such as a gymnasium floor or playing field. Participants should also be encouraged to stay hydrated by drinking water before, during, and after every workout.

Offer Coaching Cues. Timely coaching cues are the keys to success for any youth conditioning program. Moreover, effective coaching cues can help to reduce the likelihood of a training-related injury. Use coaching cues to motivate and educate during a workout. While coaching cues can be used to correct body position (e.g., "Keep your heels on the ground during the squat"), they can also be used to encourage a desirable behavior (e.g., "That's the way to 'pop' off the ground during a double-leg hop").

Provide Immediate Feedback. Help children learn to recognize what they are doing right or wrong. Kids who are aware of their mistakes will be more likely to perform the exercise correctly the next time. Immediate, constructive feedback supports learning and motivates kids to try even harder. And be sure to give ample feedback to all participants, especially the newcomers.

Program with Variety. Youth will get bored if they perform the same exercise program day after day. Furthermore, chronic, repetitive stress can result in overuse injuries. Try to use a variety of different upper- and lower-body plyometric exercises in your youth programs. Not only will the participants enjoy the program, but they will be more likely to maintain the program over the long term. We make small changes in our program every week and change the exercises every two weeks to keep the kids interested and the training stimulus effective.

Have Fun. Don't overwhelm kids with too much technical information about plyometric training. Program exercises that get children excited and keep instructions short and simple. Research suggests that factors such as participation, mastery, friendships, and positive relationships with the coach or teacher all contribute to enjoyment.

Be a Positive Role Model. Boys and girls learn from what they see and hear. In most cases, the success of a youth physical-activity program is not due to fancy equipment or expensive supplies, but rather the knowledge, care, and compassion of the teacher or coach who helps the participants feeling accepted, important, and happy.

Don't Stop Learning. Talk to strength and conditioning coaches and observe local high school and college practice sessions. Read books, attend seminars, and watch videos. The National Strength and Conditioning Association (www.nsca-lift.org) can be a valuable resource for the latest research-based information on plyometric training and sports conditioning.

4

Program Design

Progressive Plyometrics Success Story

Danielle was a young high school softball player who sustained a significant injury to her right knee while playing basketball. She had torn the anterior cruciate ligament and was referred for rehabilitation. She recovered quite well, but her real success story came while training with our progressive plyometric program. Several technique errors were noted when she jumped and landed that are common to all sports. Through hard work and by following a specific plan, she was able to overcome her knee injury and return to basketball and playing softball year-round. After training with plyometrics, she increased her foot speed and began batting again—something she had missed doing for an entire season.

Since plyometrics are not designed to be a stand-alone program, our youth conditioning program includes a variety of skills and drills that are specifically designed to enhance different fitness components. Plyometrics actually work best when integrated into a multifaceted program that includes other types of training. Furthermore, we believe it is important for children and teenagers to be exposed to different types of training and actually understand the concept of a fitness workout. That is, they need to genuinely appreciate the benefits associated with strength training, plyometric training, speed training, and flexibility training.

Regardless of age and fitness ability, the key to a safe and successful program is to follow a sensible progression plan. The idea is to develop proper form and technique on relatively simple exercises in our bronze program before progressing to more advanced drills in our silver and gold levels. We used our years of experience with children and teenagers to create our bronze, silver, and gold training programs, which are consistent with the needs and abilities of boys and girls. Due to differences in growth, development, maturation, and training experience, we realize that it is virtually impossible to create a conditioning program that can meet the specific needs of every participant. Nevertheless, we used our experiences to create a program that we believe will benefit most boys and girls. When appropriate, parents, teachers, and youth coaches may need to modify selected aspects of our program to meet the specific needs and abilities of the boys and girls in their program. For example, in some cases it may be appropriate to spend three weeks at each level instead of only two weeks.

The fundamental concept of our plyometric program is that you must build a "base" upon which to apply more advanced and complex skills. This "pyramid of success" is not a new concept. The legendary UCLA basketball coach John Wooden coined the concept many years ago. In our case, the "base," or bronze level, is designed to prepare the muscles and supporting structures for more advanced training by improving strength, power, local muscular endurance, and balance in a meaningful and skillful manner. More advanced exercises at the silver and gold levels are designed to provide a more challenging stimulus to enhance these fundamental fitness abilities. It is important to understand that quality performance at the gold level requires successful completion of the bronze and silver levels. Because plyometric training is a relatively intense mode of conditioning, youth must begin with lower-intensity drills and gradually progress. This concept forms the foundation of our progressive plyometric program.

A Complete Conditioning Program

Unlike the traditional adult exercise program in which a participant may perform 30 minutes of aerobic exercise, 20 minutes of strength training, and 10 minutes of static stretching, our youth programs integrate rather than isolate fitness components. In other words, we designed our conditioning program so that different components of each workout session not only complement each other, but also work together to enhance each other. For example, the strength-building exercises prepare the body for the plyometric drills, which in turn "excite" the neuromuscular system for the demands of speed training.

Combining fitness components is not only more effective and time efficient, but also more fun for young participants who often dislike prolonged periods of monotonous training. Our program is not difficult to follow, nor does it take a lot of time. In fact, you may find our progressive program relatively easy to follow as participants progress through our bronze, silver, and gold programs. Although learning a new skill does not occur automatically, with guidance and encouragement kids will gain confidence in their abilities to perform a new skill and therefore they will be more willing and able to perform at a higher level. While there are no short cuts or gimmicks to developing fundamental fitness skills, kids who follow our program will have fun and feel good about their performances as they develop movement competence.

Ready to Train

Although the drills and activities in our program are performed in different positions, most exercises start from the standing athletic stance (Figures 4-1 and 4-2). Before beginning the bronze level exercises, take time to review the characteristics of the athletic stance to enhance training adaptations and reduce the likelihood of injury. Time spent learning what the athletic stance "feels like" is valuable for children and adolescents. Sometimes a mirror can be a useful visual aid for teaching the athletic stance.

Figure 4-1 The athletic stance is one of the foundations of success in movement and sport.

• Eyes look ahead
• Shoulders are back
• Arms are relaxed
• Chest is over the knees
• Hips drop slightly
• Lower back is slightly arched
• Knees are slightly bent
• Feet are shoulder-width apart

Figure 4-2. Characteristics of an athletic stance

Program Progression: A Balanced Approach

Many factors must be considered when designing a plyometric training program. In Chapter 3 we outlined the acute program variables that affect the design of a plyometric workout—the choice of exercise, the order of exercise, number of repetitions, training tempo, number of sets, rest periods between sets and exercises, and training intensity. In this section we describe the specific components of the bronze, silver, and gold training programs, because it is essential to begin every workout with a plan.

Figure 4-3 is our progressive plyometric program for kids. There are three levels: bronze, silver, and gold. Each level includes several strength exercises, followed by plyometric exercises, and finally, agility exercises, that we consider "plyometrics in action." We have also progressed each exercise across the levels so that exercise number 5 in the bronze, for example, becomes more difficult as exercise number 5 in the silver level, and then is most difficult as exercise number 5 in the gold level. Chapter 5 will outline each exercise in detail, provide a list of equipment needed, starting position, action of the exercise, and finally coaching points to emphasize while the youth are performing the progressive plyometric program.

Exercise Type	Bronze Level		Silver Level		Gold Level	
Week	1	2	3	4	5	6
Sets x reps	1 x 10	2 x 10	1 x 8	2 x 8	1 x 6	2 x 6
1. Strength	MB squat		Overhead squat		6-6-6 squats	
2. Strength	A-B-C push-ups		Push-ups		Offset MB push-ups	
3. Strength	Heel raise		Ankle jumps		Hexagon drill	
4. Plyometric	Jump and freeze		Hurdle hops		Single-leg cone hops	
5. Plyometric	MB crunch		MB pull-over sit-up		MB alternate toe-touches	
6. Plyometric	Backward double-leg jump and freeze		Lateral cone hops		Long jump and sprint	
7. Plyometric	Triple "X" jump		Zigzag double-leg jump drill		Single-leg zigzag drill	
8. Plyometric	MB "stuffer" flutter		MB chest pass		MB lunge chest pass	
9. Plyometric	Standing jump and reach		90-degree jump		180-degree jump and reach	
10. Plyometric	Lateral taps on medicine ball		High five drill		Cannonball jumps	
11. Plyometric	MB overhead throw		MB backward throw		MB partner push-pass	
12. Plyometric	MB single-leg dip		MB split squat		Split squat jump	
13. Plyometric	Single-leg pops		Power skipping		Alternate bounding	
14. Speed and Agility	Arrow cone drill		Clock drill		X-drill	
15. Speed and Agility	Figure "8" drill		T-Drill		Shuttle drill	

Figure 4-3. Progressive plyometric conditioning program

Prior to performing our conditioning workout, participants should perform about five to 10 minutes of dynamic warm-up activities. After sitting in school all day (or playing video games on the weekends), boys and girls need to move when they arrive to the practice session. In our programs, participants perform a variety of different warm-up protocols before each workout. For example, most of our warm-up protocols consist of a few minutes of "easy" jogging, followed by a series of dynamic body weight calisthenics to warm up their bodies and prepare their neuromuscular systems for the challenges of plyometric training. For a little variety participants may hold a lightweight medicine ball (about two pounds) and move it in different position as they jog, or hold the medicine ball during a few of the dynamic warm-up drills. When kids perform the dynamic warm-up movements (with or without a medicine ball), we encourage a longer "stick" position to strengthen the muscles when the child may be at his weakest. For example, during the side shuffle we encourage participants to hold the squat position as they shuffle to the right and left.

- Start with relatively low-intensity drills
- Wear sneakers with tied laces
- Warm up before every workout
- Train on a yielding nonskid surface
- Perform drills in an open space
- Perform every repetition with proper form
- Sensibly progress the training program
- Allow for adequate recovery between workouts

Figure 4-4. Tips for a safe plyometric workout

Within each level we have incorporated a series of movements that begin with strength-building exercises. The reason to begin with strength-building exercises is based on one of the basic tenets for advanced plyometric training—to maximize gains from plyometric training, a basic level of muscular strength is required. As such, lower- and upper-extremity strength-building exercises have been incorporated into all three levels of our plyometric program. The sensible use of strength-building exercises may be especially important for boys and girls who lack adequate strength or body mechanics to perform plyometric drills correctly. The general idea is for these movements to become "automatic" so the skill learned can be "tapped" later on when participants learn more complex movements. Although the weight of the medicine ball will vary depending upon the size and strength of each participant, children typically start with a one- or two-pound medicine ball, while adolescents typically start with a three- or four-pound medicine ball.

After the strength-building exercises are performed the muscles are ready for even greater challenges. This is when kids perform the actual plyometric drills that are designed to enhance muscular power. Remember that plyometric training refers to jumping, hopping, and throwing drills that are designed to improve the reactive ability of the neuromuscular system. Since the learning curve for youngsters is quite steep,

Figure 4-5. Our progressive plyometric program starts with exercises designed to build the strength needed to perform the plyometric and agility movements correctly.

boys and girls should master bronze-level drills quickly provided they are given proper instruction and feedback. In any case, kids need to learn what plyometric training feels like and they need to demonstrate the ability to generate maximal power. Although the skills and drills in our progressive plyometric program are designed for children and teenagers, the physiology is the same as that of adults. The basic idea is to train the neuromuscular system to react quickly and explosively.

Figure 4-6. Plyometric exercises are dynamic, powerful, and fun movements for children. Be sure that the child can perform the exercise correctly, even if it means lowering the intensity by using smaller cones, less distance, etc.

Since plyometrics need to be performed quickly and explosively, avoid the temptation to add too many exercises onto a youngster's already busy workout routine. The idea is to energize and activate boys and girls without excessive fatigue. Our program is not a body-building routine designed to enhance muscle size, but rather a creative conditioning program designed to enhance general athletic qualities in children and adolescents. The meaningful integration of plyometric exercises into a multifaceted conditioning workout is what makes our program safe, effective, time-efficient, and fun.

After the plyometric drills are done, participants perform speed drills that are designed to exploit these newly acquired abilities. Although the speed drills are relatively short (about 10 seconds), boys and girls will find them challenging as they try to do their best. After all, we define fun as a balance between skill and challenge. So as long as the drills are somewhat challenging (and not too fatiguing), participants will think the workout is fun. However, if the kids are fatigued, performance will be suboptimal and the "fun factor" will begin to fade. In short, suboptimal training will result in suboptimal gains. Coaches and teachers should allow for adequate recovery between sets and exercises and promote the idea that fitness training can be challenging and enjoyable. This is particularly important for youth since healthy habits such as physical activity tend to track into adulthood.

Figure 4-7. Agility is plyometrics in action! With adequate strength and plyometric abilities, youth can become much more agile, and this increase in agility directly translates into more success with sport skills.

Proper Progression

Right now, you might be asking yourself, "Where do I start?" The simple answer is to start at the bronze level and work your way up to the silver and gold levels. Although certain instances may arise in which a child or adolescent with strength and conditioning experience may be able to start at a higher level, we believe it is always best to err on the side of conservatism and begin at the bronze level. While some kids may be tempted to begin at a higher level, their energy and enthusiasm for training should be redirected toward developing proper form and technique on the fundamental drills in our program. Like building a house, the key is to start with a solid foundation.

Program Variation

Although most children and adolescents will be able to progress through the bronze, silver, and gold programs within a six-week period (i.e., two weeks at each level), it is most important that participants are performing the exercises with proper form and technique. If a movement is not performed correctly an injury can occur, so it is vital to observe the performance of all activities so that additional instruction and encouragement can be offered to participants who need extra help. For example, if a child is struggling to perform selected drills or simply looks "flat" while performing plyometric movements, then the child is not ready to move on to the next level. On the other hand, if a child masters the performance of all exercises quickly and has developed some "pop" in the jumping drills then the child may be ready to move to the next level after only one week. As you can see, progression to the next level should be individualized because a variety of factors including genetics, maturation, training experience, and nutrition can influence the rate at which a child adapts to the training program. However, when working with groups, the overall ability of the group has to become a consideration as the program is progressed.

For example, a child has successfully performed double-leg forward jumps during the first week of practice. From our experience, this is a drill that most children can perform with proper body mechanics and a reduced risk of injury. This child can progress to hurdle jumps over a six-inch hurdle as long as he can maintain proper body position while jumping and landing. However, if six-inch hurdle hops are performed with improper technique the child will be at an increased risk of injury. In this case, lower hurdles should be used (e.g., 3 inches) or the child should return to double-leg forward jumps. Regardless of whether the child is at the bronze, silver, or gold level, you always have the option of modifying the program by performing more advanced exercises or simply spending a longer period of time learning unfamiliar movements. Suggestions of when not to advance to the silver or gold level are outlined in Figure 4-8.

> • Lack of body control while moving
> • Prolonged contact time with the ground while jumping or hopping
> • Knees collapse inward when landing from a jump or hop
> • Hard, noisy landings
> • Subjective comments that the exercise is "too hard"

Figure 4-8. When not to progress the training program

We designed our progressive program to develop movement skills and athletic qualities in children and adolescents. Ideally, our program should be performed at least six weeks before the start of the sports season because sports medicine research suggests that this type of preseason conditioning can actually reduce the likelihood of sports-related injuries in young athletes. We realize, however, that this may not always be possible. In some cases, boys and girls enter sports programs with suboptimal levels of fundamental physical abilities. Although it may be tempting to focus entirely on the development of sport-specific skills such as kicking a soccer ball or throwing a football, we believe that every youth sports practice session should include activities to develop fundamental fitness abilities. If you do not have enough time to perform our entire program, consider the following ideas that you can use to incorporate fundamental physical activities into your youth sports program:

Begin every practice session with dynamic warm-up activities. Various fundamental movement skills that enhance movement efficiency can become a routine part of every warm-up period. Gradually progress from simple movements at a controlled speed to more complex movements characterized by faster movements. Since one goal of the warm-up is to "excite" the neuromuscular system without undue fatigue, remember to incorporate short rest periods between each warm-up activity so that each drill is performed with proper form and technique.

Perform only one set of each exercise. While multiple sets will result in greater gains, one-set training is a time-efficient way to enhance the fitness abilities of boys and girls, particularly those who are sedentary or have limited fitness-training experience. Keep in mind that not all exercises need to be performed for the same number of sets. It is acceptable to perform one set of some exercises and two sets of others.

If time constraints limit the performance of all 15 exercises at a given level, perform the odd number exercises on day one and the even number exercises on day two. This program variation will obviously take half the time of a full workout. Since each level of our program includes carefully chosen strength, plyometric, and speed drills, performing every other exercise (as opposed to performing the first seven or the last eight) will ensure that all fitness components are at least minimally trained. This type of workout may also be appropriate for young athletes who are currently participating in four or more sport-specific training sessions per week. Since these young athletes may be at an increased risk for overtraining, any additional physical demands placed on their developing bodies needs to be carefully selected. Remember that it is always better to undertrain than overtrain.

Our progressive plyometric training program is designed to provide variety, excitement and challenge to children and adolescents. This type of training should not become drudgery, nor should it be viewed as a contest in which some children win and others lose. While we recognize the fact that participants look forward to new exercises and different challenges, we are also aware that boys and girls enjoy mastering a new skill and gaining confidence in their physical abilities. When appropriate, modify our six-week program to meet the specific needs of children and adolescents in your program. However, be reasonable and make sure you provide an opportunity for all participants to learn new skills, experience success, and feel good about their accomplishments.

Summary

Designing a safe and effective youth conditioning program involves an understanding of pediatric exercise science along with an appreciation of the "art" of developing fitness programs. Our progressive bronze, silver, and gold programs consist of drills and activities that are specifically designed to enhance fundamental athletic qualities such as strength, power, speed, and agility. With appropriate guidance, coaching, and program progression, boys and girls of all abilities can become stronger, faster, and more powerful. This will prepare them for the demands of more advanced training programs later in life.

5

Bronze, Silver, and Gold Exercises

Progressive Plyometrics Success Story

Kristina, a synchronized swimmer, had so many complaints of shoulder pain and loss of function that she was about to give up the sport and walk away from it. Instead, she joined her teammates in a regular program of progressive plyometrics and was able to regain enough shoulder strength so that the pain went away and her total function returned. She continued to participate in a similar program for several years after her initial shoulder injury and eventually become a member of the U.S. Olympic Team in synchronized swimming.

Let's get started! In this chapter, we describe all of the exercises at the bronze, silver, and gold levels of our progressive plyometric program. Our plyometric exercise program includes basic strength-building exercises such as body weight squats and progresses to more complex movements including single-leg drills and agility training. Remember that it is important to perform a dynamic warm-up routine prior to performing any conditioning drill. The warm-up adequately prepares the child's muscles for the demands of physical activity, helps to focus the child's attention on the training program, and may reduce the likelihood of training-related injuries (see Chapter 4 for warm-up drills).

In addition, keep in mind that the quality of movement is far more important than the number of repetitions performed. In other words, it is better to perform six repetitions of an exercise properly than 10 repetitions with poor technique. To build a foundation for future success, youth coaches and teachers must emphasize the basics and focus on the development of proper exercise technique and remind youth that every repetition of a movement should be performed correctly with energy and vigor. While we do encourage boys and girls to do their best and at times may challenge them to exercise near the top of their comfort zone, we always remember that enjoyment of the training program and feeling good about their accomplishments is what keeps kids coming back for more. Each of the various exercises included in the bronze, silver, and gold levels of our progressive plyometrics program is explained and demonstrated in greater detail in the DVD that accompanies this book. We highly recommend that coaches, teachers, parents, and athletes use this helpful and informative DVD in conjunction with the text to enable the child to perform each exercise using the best possible technique.

Our progressive plyometric program does not require a lot of special equipment. A few cones and medicine balls are all that you need (see Appendix B for equipment resources). And even if you don't have access to cones and medicine balls you can get a little creative and use soccer balls and other items to make our program work. If you have access to a sports field with permanent lines you may not even need cones because the distance between the lines can be used for specific drills. Above all, the key is to create an exercise environment and use training equipment that is safe and appropriate for children.

Regardless of prior sport experience, youth should start our program at the bronze level and progress to the silver and gold levels only as technique and confidence improve. We designed our progressive plyometric program to be just that—progressive! As such, begin with relatively simple movements and gradually progress to more advanced exercises so that participants experience success early on and gain confidence in their abilities to perform plyometric drills. As suggested throughout this text, keep in mind that our program is designed as a foundation from which you can add or delete exercises, depending on your participants' specific needs and the time available for training. You can choose other exercises or design other combinations of drills to meet the needs and abilities of youth in your program. However, regardless of

When available, use the lines or markings on the field or court for the start and stop points for our progressive plyometric program. These lines never move and so provide the coach with consistent distances for a particular exercise, and the kids don't have to worry about placing the cones back in position after they are moved or knocked over.

the athletic abilities of the participants, we cannot overemphasize the importance of developing proper exercise technique, gradually progressing the training program, and providing an opportunity for all participants to feel good about their performance.

In this chapter, all of the exercises are grouped into one of three categories—the bronze, silver, and gold levels. Use the following format to explain and demonstrate each exercise:

- Name of the exercise
- Diagram or picture showing the exercise
- Equipment needed for the exercise
- Description of the exercise movement
- Coaching points to keep the exercise safe and effective

Bronze Level Exercises

Bronze Exercise #1: Medicine Ball Squat

Equipment Needed: Medicine ball or sport-specific ball

Start:
- Stand tall with your feet shoulder-width apart and hold a medicine ball against your chest.
- Keep the head up and look forward.

Action:
- Move the hips backward and downward until the knees are bent 90 degrees, like sitting back in a chair. Try to keep the knees over or behind the toes. Note: If the child cannot perform a full squat (90 degrees) with proper form, start with a partial squat until they are able to move through a full range of motion.
- Return to the starting position and repeat.

Coaching Points:
- Have the exerciser keep the head in the neutral position, looking eight to 10 feet ahead.
- The low-back should be slightly arched and both heels should remain on the ground.
- Do not allow the exerciser to "bounce" out of the bottom position.
- Teach the participants to move in a controlled manner when going down and accelerate when going up.

Bronze Exercise #2: A-B-C Push-Up

Equipment Needed: None

Start:
- Start in the traditional push-up position with both arms extended and both feet on the ground.

Action:
- While maintaining a rigid body position, lift the right hand to touch the chest then return the right hand to the ground.
- Repeat with the left hand and alternate until the desired number of repetitions is complete.

Coaching Point:
- Have the exerciser avoid twisting to the right and left as the hands are lifted off the ground.

Bronze Exercise #3: Heel Raise

Equipment Needed: None

Start:
- Stand near a wall or partner with your feet shoulder-width apart. Hold onto the wall or a partner's shoulder for balance.

Action:
- While keeping the toes on the ground and the legs straight, lift the heels off the ground as high as possible in a controlled manner.
- Lower the heels to the ground in a controlled motion and repeat.

Coaching Points:
- The exerciser should move in a controlled motion in both directions.
- Emphasize lifting the heels as high as possible.

Bronze Exercise #4: Jump and Freeze

Equipment Needed: None

Start:
• Stand tall with the feet shoulder-width apart.

Action:
• Bend at the knees and quickly jump as far forward as possible. Immediately upon touching down, freeze and hold the position for three to five seconds. Repeat for the desired number of repetitions.
• Use both arms to assist in the forward jumping movement.
• Land with both knees slightly bent.
• Perform each jump explosively.

Coaching Points:
• Both feet should land on the ground at the same time.
• Have the exerciser bend at the knees to land "softly."
• Teach the participants to maintain control of the upper body and trunk during takeoff and landing.

Bronze Exercise #5: Medicine Ball Crunch

Equipment Needed: Medicine ball or sport-specific ball

Start:
- Lie on your back with both knees bent at a 90-degree angle. Hold the ball between your knees and squeeze gently (or lift both feet off the ground and place the ball on your shins).
- Place both hands on your thighs.

Action:
- While holding your head in a neutral position, lift the shoulder blades off the ground as you reach both hands toward the ball. Try to touch the ball while keeping your lower back on the ground.
- Pause briefly, then lower your body back to the ground and repeat for the desired number of repetitions.

Coaching Points:
- Have the exerciser look at the ball during the movement to keep the head in a desirable position.
- The exercise should not jerk the head or shoulders off the floor.
- Teach the participants to move in a controlled manner in both directions.

Bronze Exercise #6: Backward Double-Leg Jump and Freeze

Equipment Needed: None

Start:
- Stand with your feet shoulder-width apart, chest over the knees, arms at your sides, and elbows bent 90 degrees.

Action:
- Bend at the knees and jump backward.
- Use quick double-arm actions, keeping the elbows at 90 degrees for body control.
- Immediately upon touching down, freeze for three to five seconds and then repeat.
- Try to keep your chest over the toes as much as possible to avoid falling backward.

Coaching Point:
- Emphasize control of the jump rather than the distance of the jump.

Bronze Exercise #7: Triple "X" Jump

Equipment Needed: Three three-inch-high disc cones aligned 12 inches apart

Start:
• Stand with your feet shoulder-width apart about 12 inches to the left of the first cone.

Action:
• Bend at the knees and jump diagonally over the second cone, with both feet landing about 12 inches to the right of the third cone.
• Immediately upon touching down, jump to the left over the third cone.
• Then jump diagonally backward over the second cone and land to the right of the first cone.
• Jump laterally to the left over the first cone, back to the starting position.
• One repetition is a complete rotation consisting of four total jumps.

Coaching Points:
• The exerciser should always face forward as he jumps over the cones.
• Alternate starting at the right or left of the first cone with each set.
• Have the exerciser land softly and jump explosively spending as little time on ground as possible.
• Emphasize the height of each jump as skill and strength/power improve.

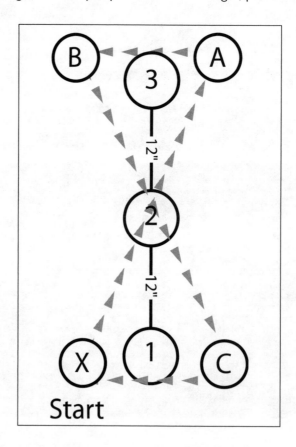

Bronze Exercise #8: Medicine Ball "Stuffer" Flutter

Equipment Needed: Medicine ball or sport-specific ball

Start:
- While in a push-up position, place both hands on a medicine ball and keep both arms straight, the back flat, and the feet wider than shoulder-width apart.

Action:
- While maintaining an erect body position with the legs extended, lift your right leg two to four inches off the ground.
- Return to the starting position and repeat with the other leg for the desired number of repetitions.

Coaching Points:
- Emphasize keeping pressure on the medicine ball while moving the legs.
- Have the exerciser maintain a rigid body position and avoid turning to the right and left as the legs are lifted.
- A leather medicine ball will make it easier to maintain balance on the ball.
- This exercise can also be performed with both hands on the ground.

Bronze Exercise #9: Standing Jump and Reach

Equipment Needed: Medicine ball or sport-specific ball (optional)

Start:
- Stand with the feet shoulder-width apart and both arms fully extended overhead.

Action:
- Bend your knees and explode upward, reaching as high as possible overhead.
- Land "softly" with the knees bent and repeat for the desired number of repetitions.

Coaching Points:
- After the exerciser bends her knees, she should rapidly explode upward to maximize the height of each jump.
- Landing softly by bending the knees allows the exerciser to "reload" for the next jump.
- For a more challenging drill, have a partner toss a ball in the air as the exerciser jumps, so she has a target to reach toward.

Bronze Exercise #10: Lateral Taps on Medicine Ball

Equipment Needed: Medicine ball or sport-specific ball

Start:
- Stand with one foot on the medicine ball and the other to the side of the ball on the ground. Keep both arms extended out to your sides and parallel to the ground.

Action:
- Hop laterally over the ball while tapping the top of the ball with the inside foot. Keep the arms parallel to the ground during the movement.
- Hop back in the reverse direction and repeat for the desired number of repetitions.

Coaching Points:
- Make sure the ball is secure on the ground to prevent rolling.
- Have the exerciser focus on rapidly moving each foot onto and off of the ball.
- To learn this drill, the exerciser can begin by looking at the ball and his feet while completing the drill.
- Over time, the exerciser should try to perform this drill while looking forward.

Bronze Exercise #11: Medicine Ball Overhead Throw

Equipment Needed: Medicine ball or sport-specific ball

Start:
• Hold a medicine ball with both hands and move it to the starting position behind the back of the head.

Action:
• Take one step forward and throw the medicine ball as far forward as possible toward a partner.

Coaching Points:
• Have the exerciser throw the medicine ball with both hands and avoid one-hand "baseball" throws.
• Teach the participants to try and use the upper- and lower-body to maximize the distance of each throw.
• The ball should bounce and roll before it reaches the partner.

Bronze Exercise #12: Medicine Ball Single-Leg Dip

Equipment Needed: Medicine ball or sport-specific ball

Start:
• Balance on one leg while holding a medicine ball near your chest.

Action:
• Dip (or squat) approximately four to six inches and then return to the starting position.
• Maintain balance on one leg while completing the desired number of repetitions.

Coaching Points:
• Have the exerciser try to keep the moving knee over or behind the toes as he dips.
• Start with small movements and gradually increase the depth of the dip as strength and balance improve.
• Instruct the exerciser to keep the back slightly arched and avoid excessive forward lean.
• This exercise can also be performed without a medicine ball.

Bronze Exercise #13: Single-Leg Pops

Equipment Needed: None

Start:
- Stand comfortably with the feet shoulder-width apart and both arms bent 90 degrees.

Action:
- This exercise is an exaggerated skipping motion.
- Lift the right knee upward until the thigh is parallel to the ground. Pop off the left foot and rapidly bring the left thigh parallel to the ground as the right foot returns to the starting position. Move the left arm upward with the right knee and the right arm upward with the left knee.
- Rapidly repeat each side for the desired number for repetitions.

Coaching Points:
- The exerciser should spend as little time on the ground as possible while maintaining proper body position.
- Encourage the participants to develop a smooth, even rhythm.
- Emphasize getting the knees as high as possible.
- Teach the participants to focus on a full ankle extension with each pop.

Bronze Exercise #14: Arrow Cone Drill

Equipment Needed: Five cones

Start:
- Place the each of the five cones approximately five yards apart.

Action:
- Start at cone 1.
- Run forward and touch cone 3.
- Turn and run back to touch cone 2.
- Turn again and run forward to cone 4.
- Turn again and run back to touch cone 3.
- Turn and run past cone 5.
- Repeat for the desired number of repetitions.

Coaching Points:
- This speed and agility drill should be performed as fast as possible.
- Have the participants focus on efficiently changing direction while maintaining body control.
- Emphasize leading the movement with the eyes, head, trunk, and then legs.

Bronze Exercise #15: Figure "8" Drill

Equipment Needed: Two cones

Start:
• Place the two cones approximately 15 yards apart. Start approximately five yards behind the cone closest to you.

Action:
• Run around the first cone, cross the middle, and then run back around the second cone in the shape of a figure 8 as you return to the first cone. Repeat this pattern for the desired number of repetitions.

Coaching Points:
• Each exerciser should try to complete this drill as quickly as possible.
• Perform this drill in different directions if multiple sets are performed.
  ✓ Possible modifications for this drill include the following:
  ✓ Set up cones at different distances apart (e.g., five yards or 20 yards).
  ✓ Have the participants run while always facing the same direction when at the starting point.
  ✓ Instruct each exerciser to jump or hop three or five times over each cone before running to the next cone.
  ✓ Have the participants run a circle around each cone before running to the next cone.

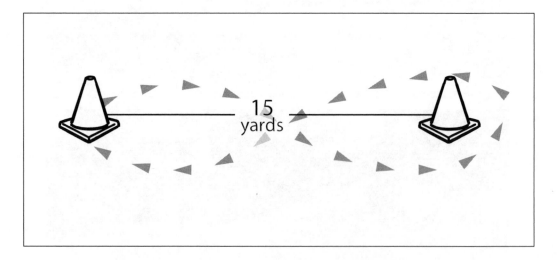

Silver Level Exercises

The 15 exercises at the silver level are designed to help youth continue their plyometric training while gradually increasing the difficulty of each exercise. As with the bronze level program, these exercises are performed for at least two weeks. Most youth will be able to learn these exercises relatively quickly because most of the silver level exercises are similar to the bronze level exercises. However, in certain circumstances, you may need to slightly modify the program to allow some children additional time to master certain movements. Therefore, as with any skill, coaches and teachers need to be "flexible" with regards to program progression to accommodate individual needs and abilities. While it is reasonable to challenge youth in your programs, progressive overload should occur in small increments. While some coaches and participants may be tempted to progress quickly, improvements will last longer if you take a little more time at each level to develop proper exercise form and technique.

With all of our exercises, it is important to perform movements in both directions to develop symmetry and body control. The focus of each drill should be on the quality of the movement to develop techniques that will be needed for more advanced exercises in the gold program as well as in sports. As the exercises become more challenging, it is important to perform each exercise correctly, even if it is performed through a partial range of motion. Once youth develop a solid foundation for plyometric training, strength, power, and speed will improve, which in turn will allow for the performance of exercises through the full range of motion as well as exercises that require more skill and coordination. As you review the exercises in this section, remember that each drill can be modified to suit the abilities of youth in your program. For example, you can change the distance between the lines or lower the height of the cones to allow all participants to perform a drill correctly. It is always better to be conservative at first and provide each child with an opportunity to perform a quality movement.

Silver Exercise #1: Overhead Squat

Equipment Needed: Medicine ball

Start:
- Stand with your feet shoulder-width apart and hold a medicine ball overhead with both arms extended.

Action:
- Keep the medicine ball overhead with arms extended throughout the movement.
- Move the hips backward and downward until the knees are at 90 degrees, like sitting back in a chair. Try to keep the knees over or behind the toes. Note: If the child cannot perform a full squat (90 degrees) with proper form, have him start with a partial squat until he is able to move through a full range of motion.
- Move in a controlled manner in each direction.
- Return to the starting position and repeat.

Coaching Points:
- Remind participants to keep both heels on the ground during the downward and upward phases and keep the knees over or behind the toes.
- Teach the exerciser to avoid excessive forward lean by maintaining a "strong" lower back.
- Participants should try to keep the medicine ball extended overhead throughout the movement.

Silver Exercise #2: Push-Ups

Equipment Needed: None

Start:
- Get in the standard push-up position with the feet apart, legs extended, and arms straight with both hands on the floor about shoulder-width apart.

Action:
- Lower the chest toward the floor by bending the elbows to approximately 90 degrees, then return to the starting position and repeat.

Coaching Points:
- Instruct the exerciser to keep the back "flat" during this exercise.
- If the child can't touch the floor with his chest, have him lower his body until the elbows are at 90 degrees.
- For variety, the hands can be arranged in different positions (e.g., hands together with thumbs touching or hands off center with one hand forward and one hand back).

If assuming a standard push-up is not possible, working from the knees is acceptable initially.

Silver Exercise #3: Ankle Jumps

Equipment Needed: None

Start:
• Stand with your feet shoulder-width apart.

Action:
• Using only the ankles to generate momentum, jump up and down continuously in one place.
• Keep the knees relatively straight, but allow them to bend slightly when landing.
• Extend the ankles to their maximum range of motion on each jump.
• Land in the same position and immediately repeat the next jump.

Coaching Points:
• The exerciser should spend as little time on the ground as possible.
• Teach the participants to use their arms to lift the body off the ground with each jump.
• Tell the participants to try to get as high as possible in the air.

Silver Exercise #4: Hurdle or Cone Jumps

Equipment Needed: Eight cones that are three to eight inches high

Start:
- Line the cones up approximately 12 to 18 inches apart.
- Stand at one end of the line of cones.

Action:
- Rapidly jump forward over each cone with both feet.
- Keep your body vertical and do not let knees "cave in" when you land.
- Use a double-arm swing to maintain balance and get more height with each jump.
- Repeat the series of jumps for the desired number of repetitions.

Coaching Points:
- Emphasize a powerful movement from the hips and knees while jumping.
- The exerciser should spend as little time on the ground as possible.
- Teach the participants to control the landing and land softly on both feet.
- Use taller cones to make this exercise more difficult.

Silver Exercise #5: Medicine Ball Pull-Over Sit-Up

Equipment Needed: Medicine ball or sport specific ball

Start:
- Lie on your back with both the hips and knees bent to 90 degrees and hold a ball behind your head with your arms bent.

Action:
- As you curl forward and lift your shoulder blades off the floor, bring the ball over your head and touch the ball just past your knees. Extend both arms if needed.
- Lower the body and the ball to the starting position and repeat.

Coaching Points:
- Instruct the exerciser to keep the lower back on the ground throughout this movement.
- The exerciser should keep his hips and knees at 90 degrees for the entire exercise.
- Remind the exerciser to exhale as he lifts his body and inhale as he lowers his body.

Silver Exercise #6: Lateral Cone Jumps

Equipment Needed: Eight cones that are three inches high

Start:
• Place the cones about 12 to 18 inches apart.
• Stand perpendicular to the line of cones with your feet shoulder-width apart.

Action:
• Jump sideways down the row of cones, landing on both feet after each jump.
• Once you clear the last cone, walk back to the start and repeat while facing the opposite direction.

Coaching Points:
• The exerciser should try to get both knees as high as possible and be quick off the ground after each landing.
• Progress to taller cones for a greater challenge.

Silver Exercise #7: Zigzag Double-Leg Jump Drill

Equipment Needed: Line on court, field, or floor

Start:
• Stand with your feet shoulder-width apart at one end of the line.

Action:
• Using your arms to help lift your body, jump up and land on the other side of the line while moving forward. Immediately repeat the jump to the other side of the line, again as far forward as possible. Each jump counts as one repetition.

Coaching Points:
• The exerciser should spend as little time on the ground as possible.
• Encourage the exerciser to try to jump as far down the line as possible.

Silver Exercise #8: Medicine Ball Chest Pass

Equipment Needed: Medicine ball

Start:
• Sit on the ground with your knees bent, feet on the floor, and a ball in your hands at chest level.
• Your partner should be facing you in the same position about 10 feet away.

Action:
• Explosively push the ball upward (at a 45-degree angle) off your chest toward your partner.
• The partner catches the medicine ball and brings it to his chest before quickly passing it back to you.

Coaching Points:
• Remind both participants to extend both arms as they pass the ball.
• After catching the ball, the exercisers must return it to their chests before passing it.
• Instruct the participants to always look at their partner and keep both hands in the "open" ready position.

Silver Exercise #9: 90-Degree Jump

Equipment Needed: None

Start:

- Stand with your feet about shoulder-width apart. Face an object as a point of reference.

Action:

- Jump up as high as you can, using your arms to help, and while in the air turn 90 degrees to the right. Land and immediately repeat the jump, turning 90 degrees back to the left so that you are back in the starting position. Repeat for the desired number of repetitions. Each jump counts as one repetition.

Coaching Points:

- For the second set, the exerciser should begin by jumping to the left.
- Remind the participants to land with "soft" knees and proper body control.
- The exerciser should spend as little time on the ground as possible while maintaining good balance.
- This drill should be performed as rapidly as possible.

Silver Exercise #10: High Five Drill

Equipment Needed: None needed, but a partner is helpful

Start:
• Stand with your feet shoulder-width apart about three feet away from a partner.

Action:
• Bend at the knees and ankles, explode up into the air as high as possible (together if done with partner), and reach one hand up and touch hands together.
• Land in a controlled manner with "soft" knees, and immediately jump up again as high as possible and touch hands.
• If a partner is not available, perform this exercise by jumping as high as possible while reaching up with one arm.

Coaching Point:
• Remind the participants to be quick off the ground and reach up as high as possible.

Silver Exercise #11: Medicine Ball Backward Throw

Equipment Needed: Medicine ball

Start:
- Stand with your feet shoulder-width apart, legs straight. and arms holding a medicine ball near your torso.

Action:
- Bend both knees and lower your body. Then, quickly explode straight up and throw the medicine ball over your head as far backward as possible.
- A partner should be positioned far enough away so that the ball can land and roll toward him. The partner should not try to catch the ball.

Coaching Point:
- The exerciser should try to get full body extension at the ankles, knees, and hips with every throw.

Silver Exercise #12: Medicine Ball Split Squat

Equipment Needed: Medicine ball

Start:
- Stand with your feet about two to three feet apart in a lunge position with the left leg forward and the knee positioned over the ankle.
- Keep the back foot on the toes and the front foot flat on the floor.
- Hold a medicine ball against your chest.

Action:
- Slowly lower your hips so that the front thigh becomes parallel with the floor and the back knee almost touches the ground. Then return to the starting position.
- Repeat for the desired number of repetitions, and then move the opposite foot forward and repeat for an equal number of repetitions.

Coaching Points:
- Remind the exerciser to maintain balance and keep the back straight at all times.
- The exerciser should avoid hitting the back knee on the ground as he lowers his body.
- For added challenge, the exerciser can hold the medicine ball behind the head and on the neck.

Silver Exercise #13: Power Skipping

Equipment Needed: None

Start:
• Stand with your feet comfortably apart.

Action:
• Hold both arms at your sides at a 90-degree angle. Move forward in a skipping motion while raising the lead knee towards your chest. Try to touch the foot with both hands.
• Repeat the motion with the opposite leg and continue skipping for 15 to 20 yards.
• Stop and repeat while going the other direction.

Coaching Points:
• Have the participants focus on touching the foot to the outstretched hands and getting the forward knee as high as possible with each skip.
• The exerciser should spend as little time on the ground as possible.
• Encourage good extension and power at the ankles, knees, and hips with each skip.

Silver Exercise #14: Clock Drill

Equipment Needed: Six cones placed five yards apart in a clockwise pattern, with cones at the 12, 2, 4, 6, 8, and 10 o'clock positions

Start:
• Stand in the middle of the circle in the "athletic position."

Action:
• Sprint forward to the 12 o'clock cone and touch the cone with one hand.
• Turn and sprint back to the middle, and then sprint to the 2 o'clock cone.
• Continue this drill by sprinting to all cones and returning to the center after touching each cone.

Coaching Points:
• Encourage the participants to focus on accelerating, decelerating, and changing direction as quickly and as efficiently as possible.
• Each exerciser should move his feet as quickly as possible between each cone.
• Modify the distance between cones based on skill and speed level.

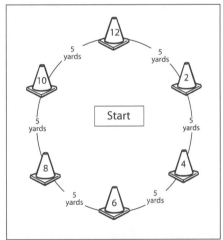

Silver Exercise #15: T-Drill

Equipment Needed: Four cones—place three cones in a row with about five yards of separation between each cone, then set one cone about 10 yards in front of the middle cone to form a "T" shape.

Start:
• Stand near the front cone in the "athletic position."

Action:
• Sprint forward to the middle cone. Shuffle to the cone on the left, then shuffle to the cone on the far right, then shuffle left back to the middle cone, and then backpedal to the starting cone.

Coaching Points:
• The exerciser should try to decelerate and change direction as quickly as possible between cones.
• Teach the participants not to cross their feet as they shuffle between cones.
• When backpedaling, the exerciser must keep his chest over the knees.
• Possible modifications for this drill include the following:
   ✓Vary the distance between cones.
   ✓Have the exerciser hop over each cone or run a circle around each cone before moving to next cone.

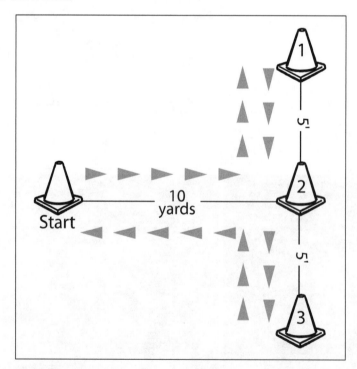

Gold Level Exercises

These exercises are the most advanced and are specifically designed for boys and girls who have developed confidence and competence in our bronze and silver level exercises. The idea is to gradually progress the intensity of the exercise program so that training adaptations continue to occur.

Gold Exercise #1: 6-6-6 Squats

Equipment Needed: Medicine ball

Start:
- Stand with your feet shoulder-width apart and hold a medicine ball against your chest. (For more advanced athletes, hold the medicine ball behind the neck, as illustrated.)

Action:
- Perform six regular squats in a controlled manner. Squat until your thighs are parallel to ground.
- Perform six "drop squats" by dropping into the full squat position then quickly exploding upward to the starting position.
- Finish the set by performing six squat jumps.

Coaching Points:
- Children should start with a two-pound medicine ball, while teenagers may progress to a four-pound ball.
- Remind the exerciser to try to keep the knees over or behind the toes during the squat.
- Do not allow the exerciser to collapse the knees inward when landing from a drop squat.

Gold Exercise #2: Offset Medicine Ball Push-Ups

Equipment Needed: Medicine ball or other sport-specific ball

Start:
• Get in the standard push-up position with your feet apart, legs extended, and arms straight. Place one hand on the floor and the other on a medicine ball.

Action:
• Slowly lower your chest toward the floor by bending both elbows, then return to the starting position by pushing off the floor and the ball. Repeat for the desired number of repetitions, then place the medicine ball under the opposite hand and repeat the drill.

Coaching Points:
• Encourage the exerciser to keep the body straight throughout the performance of each repetition.
• Use a ball not larger than a soccer ball to allow for greater range of motion.

Gold Exercise #3: Hexagon Drill

Equipment Needed: Six strips of tape (each strip 24 inches long), placed in the shape of a hexagon

Start:
• Start in the center of the hexagon in the athletic position.

Action:
• Jump straight ahead over the forward line, then immediately jump back to the starting position. While looking forward, jump over each line of the hexagon and then back to the middle. One repetition of this exercise consists of two times around the hexagon.

Coaching Points:
• The exerciser should spend as little time on the ground as possible.
• This drill should be completed as quickly as possible while maintaining good form.
• If multiple sets are performed, have the exerciser perform the second set moving in the opposite direction around the hexagon.

Gold Exercise #4: Single-Leg Cone Hops

Equipment Needed: Six disc cones placed 18 to 24 inches apart in a straight line

Start:
• Stand on one leg at one end of the cone line.

Action:
• Push off the standing leg and hop forward, landing on the same leg. Upon landing, immediately take off again and continue to hop over all of the cones. Use a strong arm swing to increase jump height and distance. At the end of the cone line, walk back to the starting position and repeat using the other leg.

Coaching Points:
• The exerciser should spend as little time as possible on the ground between the cones.
• Encourage the participants to use their upper body for balance and power as they hop over each cone.
• The participants should work toward increasing their speed through the cones while maintaining good form.

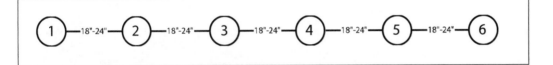

Gold Exercise #5: Medicine Ball Alternate Toe-Touches

Equipment Needed: Medicine ball or sport-specific ball

Start:
• Lie flat on your back while holding the ball overhead with both elbows bent. The knees should be bent and the feet on the ground.

Action:
• Bend your right knee and bring it toward your chest while lifting the medicine ball forward so that the medicine ball goes over the top of the right knee and touches the right foot.
• Return to the starting position and repeat with the left knee.
• Keep your lower back on the ground throughout this exercise.

Coaching Points:
• Teach the participants to exhale as they lift their shoulders off the ground. Do not allow them to hold their breath.
• Due to differences in body size and limb length, some children may not be able to touch the ball to their foot. They should simply reach as far as they can while keeping the lower back on the floor.
• Encourage each exerciser to perform this movement in a controlled and fluid motion while maintaining good form.

Gold Exercise #6: Long Jump and Sprint

Equipment Needed: Two cones placed about 15 yards apart

Start:

• Stand next to one cone with your feet shoulder-width apart.

Action:

• Using a big arm swing, long jump as far as possible. Upon landing with both feet together, immediately sprint forward to the second cone.

• Walk back to the starting position and repeat for the desired number of repetitions.

Coaching Point:

• Each exerciser should work toward jumping as far as possible while maintaining proper form.

Gold Exercise #7: Single-Leg Zigzag Drill

Equipment Needed: A line 10 yards long

Start:
• Stand on one foot to the side of the line near one end.

Action:
• Hop on one leg back and forth over the line as you move forward. Do not "double hop" at the touchdown.
• When finished, walk back to the start and repeat on the opposite leg to complete one set.

Coaching Points:
• The exerciser should spend as little time on the ground as possible.
• Encourage the participants to try to get as high and as far forward as possible with each hop.

Gold Exercise #8: Medicine Ball Lunge Chest Pass

Equipment Needed: Medicine ball and partner

Start:
- Hold a medicine ball in front of your chest while standing about 10 feet from a partner.

Action:
- While lunging forward onto one foot, quickly pass the ball off your chest to your partner.
- The partner catches the ball while stepping backward with one leg (reverse lunge), then lunges forward while quickly passing it back.

Coaching Points:
- Have the exercisers explode the ball off their chests and try to pass it as far as possible. If necessary, modify the distance between the partners.
- Remind the exercisers to keep their hands in the ready "open" position and catch the ball with "soft hands".
- To increase the challenge of this exercise, have the participants lunge forward each time with alternate legs.

Gold Exercise #9: 180-Degree Jump and Reach

Equipment Needed: None

Start:
• Stand with your feet shoulder-width apart in the athletic position and face an object as a point of reference.

Action:
• Jump as high as possible and turn 180 degrees so that you are facing the opposite direction when you land. Upon landing, immediately jump up and turn 180 degrees in the reverse direction so that you land in the starting position. Perform for the desired number of repetitions (each jump counts as one repetition).

Coaching Points:
• The exerciser should jump and land with both feet.
• Encourage the participants to use their upper body for balance as they jump and land.
• The turn should be initiated from the ground.
• Each exerciser should work toward jumping as high as possible while maintaining good form.
• If a second set is performed, the exerciser should jump in the opposite direction.

Gold Exercise #10: Cannonball Jumps

Equipment Needed: None

Start:
- Stand in the athletic position with your feet shoulder-width apart.

Action:
- Jump up as high as possible while attempting to bring both knees toward your chest (or at least bring the thighs parallel to the ground).
- Touch the knees with your hands at the highest point before returning to the ground.
- Quickly jump again and repeat for the desired number of repetitions.

Coaching Points:
- Encourage the participants to land with "soft" knees and get off the ground as quickly as possible.
- Each exerciser should work toward bringing the knees as high as possible.

Gold Exercise #11: Medicine Ball Partner Push-Pass

Equipment Needed: Medicine ball and partner

Start:
- Hold a medicine ball at chest level with your feet shoulder-width apart.

Action:
- Squat down to the ready position (about 140-degree knee bend), then quickly explode upward, lifting your body off the ground, extending both arms, and pushing the ball in an arc toward your partner, who is standing a safe distance away.
- After the ball lands, the partner retrieves it and repeats the drill in the same manner.
- Repeat and perform for the desired number of repetitions.

Coaching Points:
- The ball should land and roll after each throw. Do not allow anyone to try to catch it.
- After the squat, the exerciser should explode upward as fast and high as possible.
- Teach the participants to pass the ball at a 45-degree angle from their chests in an arc.

Gold Exercise #12: Split Squat Jump

Equipment Needed: None

Start:
• Stand in a lunge position with the front knee at 90 degrees.

Action:
• Jump using both arms to help lift while holding the split squat position.
• Land in the same position and immediately repeat the jump for the desired number of repetitions.
• Repeat with the other leg in the front position.

Coaching Points:
• Encourage each exerciser to try for complete extension of the legs and hips while jumping.
• The exerciser should push off the ground for more upward extension and try to get as high as possible with every jump.

Gold Exercise #13: Alternate Bounding

Equipment Needed: None

Start:
- Jog at a moderate pace to increase forward momentum. Start the drill with the right foot forward and left foot back.

Action:
- This drill is an exaggeration of running. Push off with the left foot and bring the right leg forward with the knee bent and the thigh parallel to the ground. At the same time, reach forward with the left arm. As the right leg comes through, the left leg extends back and remains extended. Hold this extended position for a brief time (hang time), then land on the right foot. The left leg then drives through to the front with the knee bent to the thigh-high position as the right arm reaches forward.
- Repeat for six cycles (one cycle consists of both the right and left knee coming forward). Try to cover as much distance as possible with each long stride.

Coaching Points:
- Have the exerciser accentuate pushing off the ground with the rear leg and foot and lifting the thigh parallel as the knee goes through.
- Encourage each exerciser to try to develop "hang time."

Gold Exercise #14: X-Drill

Equipment Needed: Four cones placed in a square with about five yards separating each. The cones are numbered 1 to 4, as follows: 1=bottom right, 2=top left, 3=top right, and 4=bottom left (see diagram).

Start:
- Stand in the athletic position near cone 1. Throughout this drill the athlete will look forward (in the direction of the arrow in the diagram) even though he will be running in different directions.

Action:
- Starting at cone 1, turn and run to cone 2 while looking forward.
- Plant the foot and drive sideways, shuffling to cone 3.
- Turn and run diagonally to cone 4.
- Plant the foot and drive sideways, shuffling back to cone 1.
- Repeat the entire sequence a second time without rest. These two repetitions of the sequence are considered one set of this exercise.

Coaching Points:
- Encourage the exerciser to keep his feet moving as fast as possible.
- Emphasize decelerating and then quickly accelerating.
- Tell each exerciser, "Stay on track by looking back!"

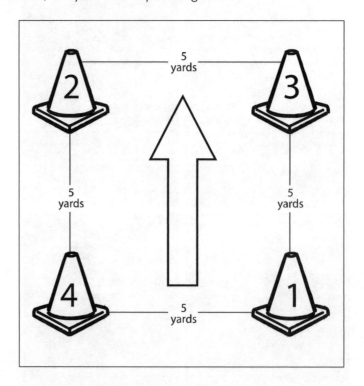

Gold Exercise #15: Shuttle Drill

Equipment Needed: Three cones placed in a line with about five yards separating each

Start:
• Stand in the athletic position next to cone 1.

Action:
• Sprint to cone 2, touch the cone, then sprint back to cone 1. Turn and sprint to cone 3, touch the cone, then turn and sprint back to cone 1 again. Repeat the entire sequence. One set consists of two complete cycles.

Coaching Points:
• Emphasize accelerating, decelerating, changing direction, and accelerating again.
• The exerciser should cut and change directions as quickly as possible.
• Teach the participants to use short "chop steps" for better body control during the deceleration as they stop and change directions.
• Each exerciser should work toward completing the drill as quickly as possible while maintaining good form.

Beyond the Gold Level

Once a youngster has successfully completed our gold level program, you should continue to make modifications to his plyometric program to keep the training regimen fresh and effective. The following are some simple ways to make your program more challenging for the child or adolescent who has completed the gold level exercises.

- Decrease the time it takes to complete each set by performing each exercise more explosively.
- Decrease the length of the rest interval between exercises, provided that this does not interfere with the technical performance of each exercise.
- Increase the distance between cones or increase the height of the cones.
- Increase the "relative weight" the participant must move during each exercise. This can be done by using heavier medicine balls (4 lbs for children or 6 lbs for adolescents) or by wearing a weighted vest while performing selected drills. By wearing a vest with added weight (less than 10% of body weight), participants will be able to perform each drill with a resistance that is heavier than their own body weight. While this type of training can be beneficial for young athletes, we suggest that youth develop a solid foundation of strength and fitness before they perform plyometric movements with added weight.

For those athletes and coaches who want to progress the intensity of our program using a weighted vest, we recommend the Xvest (see Appendix B for information and Web site).

The Xvest is an excellent training tool that can be used to increase the resistance and intensity of our progressive plyometric exercises. Resistance can be increased in one-pound increments by adding weight to the pockets around the vest.

The Xvest can also be adjusted to fit securely around the chest so that the Xvest stays in place while the child is exercising. The Xvest also comes in a variety of sizes so that each athlete can get the correct vest for her body size.

The Xvest can be used effectively during all of our running and agility exercises.

Because the Xvest can be adjusted to fit securely around the chest, it can be used effectively during any of our jumping and plyometric exercises

A

American College of Sports Medicine • Current Comment • December 2001

Plyometric Training for Children and Adolescents

Written for the American College of Sports Medicine by Avery D. Faigenbaum, Ed.D. and Donald A. Chu, Ph.D., PT, ATC

Children and adolescents need to participate regularly in physical activities that enhance and maintain cardiovascular and musculoskeletal health. While boys and girls have traditionally been encouraged to participate in aerobic training and strength building activities, a growing number of children and adolescents are experiencing the benefits of plyometric training. Plyometrics refer to exercises that link strength with speed of movement to produce power and were first known simply as "jump training." Previously thought of as a method of conditioning reserved for adult athletes, the American College of Sports Medicine (ACSM) contends that plyometric training is a safe, beneficial and fun activity for children and adolescents provided that the program is properly designed and supervised.

Plyometric training conditions the body through dynamic, resistance exercises. This type of training typically includes hops and jumps that exploit the muscles' cycle of lengthening and shortening to increase muscle power. Plyometric exercises start with a rapid stretch of a muscle (eccentric phase) and are followed by a rapid shortening of the same muscle (concentric phase). With plyometric training, the nervous system is conditioned to react more quickly to the stretch-shortening cycle.

This type of training enhances a child's ability to increase speed of movement and improve power production. Regular participation in a plyometric training program may also help to strengthen bone and facilitate weight control. Further, plyometric training performed during the preseason may decrease the risk of sports-related injuries. This may be of particular benefit to young female athletes who appear to be at increased risk for knee injuries as compared to young male athletes.

There are thousands of plyometric exercises, ranging from low intensity double leg hops to high intensity drills such as depth jumps. Although the latter is typically associated with plyometric training for the mature athlete, common games and activities such as hopscotch, jumping rope and jumping jacks can also be characterized as plyometrics because every time the feet make contact with the ground the quadriceps are subjected to the stretch-shortening cycle. In fact, plyometrics are a natural part of most movements, as evidenced by the jumping, hopping and skipping seen on any school playground.

With qualified coaching and age-appropriate instruction, plyometric training can be a safe, effective and fun method of conditioning for children and teenagers. However, there is the potential for injury to occur if the intensity and volume of the training program exceeds the abilities of the participants. Children and adolescents should develop an adequate baseline of strength before participating in a plyometric training program, or they should simply begin plyometric training with lower intensity drills and gradually progress to higher intensity drills over time.

Although additional clinical trials are needed to determine the most effective plyometric training program for children and adolescents, beginning with one to three sets of six to 10 repetitions on one upper body exercise (e.g., medicine ball chest pass with a one-kilogram ball) and one lower body exercise (e.g. double leg hop) twice per week on nonconsecutive days seems reasonable. If multiple sets are performed, participants must be provided with adequate rest and recovery between sets (e.g., two to four minutes) in order to replenish the energy necessary to perform the next series of repetitions with the same intensity. Unlike traditional strength training exercises, plyometric exercises are performed quickly and explosively. Plyometric exercises may be introduced into the warm-up period or incorporated into group game activities.

Depending upon individual needs and goals, the plyometric training program can progress to include multiple jumps, single leg hops and throws using lightweight medicine balls. Modifying the program over time will help to optimize gains and prevent overtraining. Children and adolescents should be provided with specific information on proper exercise technique, rate of progression and safe training procedures (e.g., warm-up and cool-down). Also, children and adolescents must wear supportive athletic footwear and plyometric exercises should be performed on surfaces with some resilience. Plyometrics are not intended to be a stand-alone exercise program and should be incorporated into a well-designed overall conditioning program that also includes strength, aerobic, flexibility, and agility training.

Plyometric training may not only make children and adolescents faster and more powerful; this type of training may offer observable health benefit to young populations. The contention that plyometrics are inappropriate for boys and girls is not consistent with the needs of children and teenagers or their physical abilities. Plyometric training is a safe, worthwhile and fun method of conditioning for children and adolescents if age-appropriate guidelines are followed, qualified instruction is available, and individual concerns are addressed.

Reprinted with permission of the American College of Sports Medicine, "Plyometric Training for Children and Adolescents," December 2001, www.acsm.org

B

Selected Websites and References

Selected Websites:

www.TheXvest.com
Mention promotion code PLYO3 when ordering. The Xvest can provide gradual increases in resistance while providing the athlete with a novel, secure training tool that can be used to enhance performance.

www.donchu.com
Articles available for download on selected plyometric training. Medicine balls and related fitness products are available as well.

www.nsca-lift.org
The National Strength and Conditioning Association is a professional organization offering membership, conferences, articles, and scientific publications on strength and conditioning.

www.acsm.org
The American College of Sports Medicine is a professional organization offering membership, conferences, articles, and scientific publications on sports medicine, fitness, and conditioning.

www.strongkid.com
Articles available for download on fitness and conditioning for children and teenagers.

www.performbetter.com
Fitness equipment company with a wide variety of fitness products including medicine balls, agility tools, fitness bands, and other products

www.power-systems.com
Fitness equipment company with a wide variety of fitness products including medicine balls, agility tools, fitness bands, and other products

Selected References:

American Academy of Pediatrics, Committee on Sports Medicine and Fitness. 2000. Intensive training and sports specialization in young athletes. Pediatrics, 106: 154–157.

Chu, D. 1996. *Explosive Power and Strength*. Champaign, IL. Human Kinetics.

Chu, D. 1986. *Plyoplay for Kids*. Livermore, CA. Bittersweet Publishing.

Chu, D. 1998. *Jumping Into Plyometrics*, 2nd edition. Champaign, IL. Human Kinetics.

Chu, D. 2003. *Plyometric Exercises with the Medicine Ball*, 2nd edition. Livermore, CA. Bittersweet Publishing.

Faigenbaum, A. 2001. Preseason conditioning for high school athletes. *Strength and Conditioning*, 23 (1): 70–72.

Faigenbaum, A. 2001. Strength training and children's health. *Journal of Physical Education Recreation and Dance*, 72 (3): 24–30.

Faigenbaum, A., Bellucci, M., Bernieri, A., Bakker, B., Hoorens, K. 2005. Effects of different warm-up protocols on fitness performance in children. *Journal of Strength and Conditioning Research*, 19(2):, 376–381.

Faigenbaum, A., & Chu, D. 2001. Plyometric training for children and adolescents. ACSM *Current Comment*. Published by the American College of Sports Medicine, December.

Faigenbaum, A., Kraemer, W., Cahill, B., et al. 1996. Youth resistance training: Position statement paper and literature review. *Strength and Conditioning*, 18, 62–75.

Faigenbaum, A., and Micheli, L. 2000. Preseason conditioning for the preadolescent athlete. *Pediatric Annals*. 29:156–161.

Faigenbaum, A and Schram, J. 2004. Can resistance training reduce injuries in youth sports? *Strength and Conditioning Journal*. 26, 16–21.

Faigenbaum, A. and Westcott, W. 2000. *Strength and Power for Young Athletes*; Champaign, IL. Human Kinetics.

Heidt, R., Sweeterman, L., Carlonas, R., Traub, J., Tekulve, F. 2000. Avoidance of soccer injuries with preseason conditioning. *American Journal of Sports Medicine*. 28 (5): 659–662.

Hewett, T., Stroupe, A., Nance, T., Noyes, F. 1996. Plyometric training in females athletes. *American Journal of Sports Medicine*. 24 (6): 765–773.

Hewett, T., Lindenfeld, T., Riccobene, J., et al. 1999. The effect of neuromuscular training on the incidence of knee injury in female athletes. *American Journal of Sports Medicine*. 27; 699–705.

Magill, R. and Anderson, D. 1995. Critical periods as optimal readiness for learning sports skills. In Smoll, F., Smith, R., ed. *Children and Youth in Sport: A Biopsychosocial Perspective*. Madison, WI. Brown and Benchmark. 57–72..

Mediate, P. and Faigenbaum, A. 2004. *Medicine Ball Training for All*. Monterey, CA. Healthy Learning.

Micheli, L. 2001. Preventing injuries in sports: What the team physician needs to know. In L. Micheli, A. Smith, N. Bachl, C. Rolf, & K. Chan, (eds). *F.I.M.S. Team Physician Manual*. Lippincott, Williams and Wilkins, China.

National Athletic Trainers Association. Minimizing the risk of injury in high school athletics, 2002. http://nata.org/publications/brochures/minimizingtherisks.htm

Rowland, T. 2005. *Children's Exercise Physiology*, 2nd edition. Champaign, IL. Human Kinetics.

Smith, A., Andrish, J., Micheli, L. 1993. The prevention of sports injuries of children and adolescents. *Medicine and Science in Sports and Exercise*. 25 (Suppl. 8): 1–7.

U.S. Department of Health and Human Services. 1996. *Physical Activity and Health: A Report of the Surgeon General*. Atlanta: U.S. Department of Health and Human Services, Centers for Disease Control and Prevention, National Center for Chronic Disease Prevention and Health Promotion.

About the Authors

Donald Chu, Ph.D., PT, ATC, CSCS, has more than 30 years of experience working with athletes of all ages in the area of performance enhancement. His work in plyometric training for the elite athlete has been presented in some of his earlier books, including *Jumping into Plyometrics* and *Explosive Strength and Power*. Both an educator and a coach, he has continued to train athletes at all levels in a wide variety of sports, including Olympians, and professional and scholarship athletes.

Avery D. Faigenbaum, Ed.D., CSCS*D, FACSM, is an associate professor in the department of health and exercise science at The College of New Jersey. He is a leading researcher and practitioner in the field of youth fitness, and has years of experience working with children and adolescents. Dr. Faigenbaum is the coauthor of four books including *Strength and Power for Young Athletes* and *Medicine Ball for All Training Handbook*. He is a Fellow of the American College of Sports Medicine and served as vice president of the National Strength and Conditioning Association.

Jeff Falkel, Ph.D., PT, CSCS*D, is a physical therapist and strength and conditioning coach with VDP Enterprises in Littleton, Colorado. For more than 25 years, he has treated, coached, and trained athletes of all ages, from the very young to elite international players. Dr. Falkel is also a strength and conditioning consultant for several military units. He is a coauthor of two books, *Total Knee Replacement and Rehabilitation: The Knee Owner's Manual*, and *SportsVision: Training for Better Performance*. He will be the chair of the National Strength and Conditioning Association Certification Commission from 2006 to 2008.